The Barn Door Is Open

The Barn Door Is Open

Frameworks and Tools for Success and Fulfillment in the Workplace

Serge Alfonse

BUSINESS EXPERT PRESS

Leader in applied, concise business books

The Barn Door Is Open: Frameworks and Tools for Success and Fulfillment in the Workplace
Copyright © Business Expert Press, LLC, 2021.

First published in 2021 by
Business Expert Press, LLC
222 East 46th Street, New York, NY 10017
www.businessexpertpress.com

ISBN-13: 978-1-95253-840-7 (paperback)
ISBN-13: 978-1-95253-841-4 (e-book)

Business Expert Press Supply and Operation Management Collection

Collection ISSN: 2156-8189 (print)
Collection ISSN: 2156-8200 (electronic)

Cover image licensed by Ingram Image, StockPhotoSecrets.com
Cover and interior design by S4Carlisle Publishing Services Private Ltd., Chennai, India

First edition: 2021

10 9 8 7 6 5 4 3 2 1

Dedication

I dedicate this book to all people who are invested in creating successful and fulfilling workplaces, engaged in building a better and more equitable world, interested in caring for one another, and, above all, are convinced that everything evolves around the value of love.

Advanced Quotes for *The Barn Door Is Open*

The Barn Door Is Open is a "*Who Moved My Cheese*" for improving your business by working smarter, not harder. Serge Alfonse takes readers on a delightful and instructive journey where the animal characters learn by doing. This farm tale parable is a "must-read" primer for business owners, managers and front-line workers seeking to solve today's complex business problems while putting people first.

–Frank Shines, Vice-President CCS Medical, MBA, Six Sigma Master Black Belt, author of *Let in But Left Out: Leadership, Faith and Knowledge in the Age of A.I., Coronavirus and Fake News*

It is often said that simplicity is the ultimate in sophistication, *The Barn Door is Open*, is very tangible proof of this claim. This story takes the reader through some of the most sophisticated and complex Business Analysis Processes with ease and simplicity. A brilliant approach that delivers understanding and application in a simple and enjoyable way.... Bravo !!

–Joe Brouillette, Founding Chairman of Delta Global Networks, Inc.

The Barn Door is Open is a unique treasure, one of those books that is quickly and easily understood by both new and seasoned professionals. For anyone interested in process improvement and fostering a positive, proactive, and engaged culture that sows the seeds of ongoing success, this book is a must read. Clever and entertaining metaphors are used to relay important concepts that "stick" with the reader. The second part of the book contains an abundance of effective tools and strategies that can be utilized immediately!

–Barb Birdt Prentice, Director Quality, Compliance & Training (Ret.), MBA

The Barn Door is Open brings lean culture to readers in a novel but easy to grasp way. Serge's style and language inspire confidence with continuous improvement tools. Adlai Stevenson said, "It is hard to lead a cavalry charge if you feel that you look funny on a horse." When readers put the book down, they come away with the conviction that they can lead the Lean charge."

–Anthony Skinner, Continuous Improvement Manager, MBA, Lean Six Sigma Master Black Belt

The Barn Door Is Open is an intelligent yet playful tale that gradually and profoundly changes the way we think about problem solving, continuous improvement, conflict resolution, and mindfulness. *The Barn Door Is Open* is an essential blueprint for anyone from the front-line worker to member of the executive team to successfully navigate through a Lean culture transformation. This book reveals how to become part of a team, part of the solution, and part of an ever-improving organization.

–Glenn Hoogerwerf, President - Software Services, Group VP, Technology Industry, Computer Science and Management degrees from Carnegie Mellon University

Abstract

The Barn Door Is Open: Frameworks and Tools for Success and Fulfillment in the Workplace is a business book, a playful read, an intelligent metaphorical tale anchored in the tools and techniques of innovative and proven management frameworks. It is also a philosophical tale that uses humor and metaphors to make the learning entertaining and inspirational. *The Barn Door Is Open* is designed to be read at multiple layers, from neophytes to seasoned professionals. While there are many hidden references that astute readers will appreciate, the concepts covered are easy to understand and implement. Self-help readers will benefit from many of its lessons and tools by applying them to their personal lives.

The Barn Door Is Open provides prescriptive, step-by-step learning points with ample hands-on examples. *The Barn Door Is Open* treats the subjects and tools of Lean and Lean Transformation, mindfulness, conflict resolution, Theory of Constraints (TOC), project management, Agile, Six Sigma, change management, and corporate culture transformation in one easily digestible reference.

All of us as students, workers, managers, executives in any business, in any industry struggle to solve problems. We lose focus. We do not look deep enough. We simply do not know how. We can be taught to think differently, leading to a higher level of reasoning, phenomenal personal growth, and a more fulfilling career. *The Barn Door Is Open* gradually and profoundly changes the way we think and lays the foundations for a successful and fulfilling workplace.

Keywords

process improvement; Lean journey; transformation to a happy and fulfilling workplace; creating a Lean culture; management tools and frameworks; problem solving; innovative use of Lean; managing conflict resolution; self-help and personal development; mindfulness at work; quality assurance; quality management; management strategies; successful workplaces; change management; organizational culture

Contents

List of Figures

List of Tables

Preface

The monolith of knowledge needs to be passed on. Sharing this knowledge is not only fulfilling but gives us a purpose in life.

Through the people and experiences we encounter on our life journey, we may choose the path to build ourselves up, to get inspired, to reach self-actualization. As the wheels of time turn, we may seize the opportunity to take the place of our teachers and mentors.

The Barn Door Is Open is the sharing of my knowledge and experiences accumulated during thousands of hours of consulting work, countless training programs taught and taken, and the fruit of failure and success.

The concept for the *Barn Door Is Open* started long before the first chapter was written. The idea incubated for several years before turning into a concrete project. On a year-long family sabbatical of travel, I was granted the gift of time. While in Namibia, overlooking a waterhole watching elephants, giraffes, and lions come and go, words started flowing. Subsequent chapters took shape as we visited the capital cities of Europe, marveling at the architectural splendors and the cultural riches. The last chapters were developed in Southeast Asia, fed by an insatiable appetite to eat delicious soups, immerse ourselves in the glory of the past, and witness the inevitable race to the future. The editing took place overlooking a Pacific Ocean lagoon on the island of New Caledonia where our stay had unexpectedly extended. From the first chapter to the last revision, this book was my constant companion throughout that year.

The greatest challenge encountered in writing the *Barn Door Is Open* was pulling together tools, management frameworks, and methods from various disciplines into one reference book that would deliver maximum value to neophyte readers and seasoned executives alike.

As we learn by doing, many examples that can be used as exercises are found peppered throughout the reading. As we learn by playing, hidden clues and humorous situations will be encountered throughout the story.

These might remind readers of some of the awkward situations and behaviors in their own past or present workplaces or personal lives.

As we have all experienced, company politics start when we add the second employee to an organization. That is, unfortunately, a pretty low threshold. *The Barn Door Is Open* teaches the lessons to create a successful and fulfilling workplace. I cannot wait for the reader to meet the various characters of this business and philosophical tale that will drive that point home.

Acknowledgments

First and foremost, my deepest gratitude goes to my life partner and wife Lyne. Without her, and her meticulous editing and rigorous critiquing, this book would not have seen the light of day. We had some heated debates as well as some good laughs as we poured through the many versions of this book.

Thank you to my daughter Camille for her patience, support, and input, and especially for coming up with the book title *The Barn Door Is Open*. An unbound child's mind can accomplish almost anything.

I have always been surrounded by the essential light of unconditional love by my Father Gerard, Mother Monique, Stepmother Daniele, Sister Natacha, and countless other family members. Their love helped guide *The Barn Door Is Open*.

My fondest appreciation to all the mentors, teachers, co-workers, and friends that offered so many learning, reflecting, and growing opportunities that in some way, shape, or form were woven into the pages of this book. A special callout goes to my friends Barb and Michelle for reading the very first draft and encouraging me to pursue this project, Tony for applying his Six Sigma and statistical skills through the different revisions of the book, and Saleem for exemplifying the value of ethics.

It is thanks to all of the people and conditions above that I was able to lay down the words of *The Barn Door Is Open*. My deepest hope is that this book will guide you to success and fulfillment.

PART 1

The Barn Door Is Open

CHAPTER 1

Building the Farm

"When was the last time you put the canoe in the water Grandpa?"

"I keep the canoe in the water all year round Granddaughter. It mostly sits idle tied to the pier waiting for its next journey."

"Who chooses the way?"

"Most of the time I am the one. Other times, it is a passenger that shapes the trip. Every so often, it is determined by the mercy of the river. Now, speaking of mercy, did you bring the marshmallows and chocolate for our overnight stop?"

"I did, graham crackers too."

"All right! The day is young, and it looks like we are all set for our adventure Granddaughter. Untie the rope, push off, and hop in!"

"It's nice being here with you Grandpa. I have so many questions for you as we paddle?"

"I didn't expect that Miss Curiosity would be able to stay silent for even a minute during this expedition. That is what I love about you. Go on, ask away."

"Grandma says you are wise."

"Grandma knows that wise is what wise does."

"What is it that you did that makes you wise?"

"You know Granddaughter, I built a farm. Anyone can build a farm for that our farms do not require brick or mortar, money or labor, or property rights. Only the fruit of one's imagination is needed."

"How big is your farm Grandpa?"

"My farm started small, with only two fields. One was fertile and green all year round. On the other side of the dirt road was the second field. I called it the bad land. Nothing grew there. Through the years, more fertile fields were added to the farm to grow more of the food that nourishes our souls."

"And the bad land, did that get bigger too?"

"At first the bad land was not fenced in on one side. Year after year, I fenced it in and kept working on shrinking its size."

"What is the bad land for?"

"There is always an infertile field on a farm. The bad land is needed to dispose of anything that renders other fields infertile. My favorite things to bury there are negative thoughts."

"What are negative thoughts?"

"Thoughts that cause you distress. Ones that are critical rather than helpful, judgmental rather than forgiving. Thoughts that take us down rather than build us up, or that are sarcastic and destructive rather than sincere and creative. Thoughts that are painful memories rather than happy ones. The most important thing to do Granddaughter is to recognize them as they form in your mind."

"After you recognize a negative thought, how do you put it in the ground?"

"There is no one method; it is for you to figure out your own way."

"Can you share your technique for burying your negative thoughts?"

"I first compress the words that make the negative thoughts in a very tight ball and wrap it with some thought leak-proof material so the words and the negative energy cannot escape. As for the burying part, I give it to a black bird if not too negative or dig the hole myself if the thought is really toxic."

"So, you have to be mean with those negative thoughts?"

"No, you have to be gentle with all your thoughts. As for the negative ones, recognize them first, acknowledge them, and then dispose of them in the bad land to make room for more fertile thoughts."

"What about other people's negative thoughts?"

"It is quite simple; they receive the same treatment: recognize, acknowledge, give a proper wrapping, and off to the burial ground in the fenced bad land they go."

"Do they ever come out of the bad land?"

"They surely do, and you have to put them right back where they belong, maybe with a different wrapper. It is key to learn to bury bad thoughts deeper in the bad land. It is more valuable for our well-being to practice *purpose thinking*, thinking with a positive purpose, rather than ruminating on bad thoughts."

"Am I too young to build my own farm Grandpa?"

"It's never too early nor too late to build your own farm. It is quite simple to get started. Close your eyes and dream of your farmhouse. Start with a fertile field, a dirt road, and a bad land."

CHAPTER 2

POUT

"Are there others on your farm Grandpa?"

"Like on all farms, 'happiness is only real when shared'[1] Granddaughter. Most of the inhabitants that stay for a while are animals and farmhands. We also have a fair number of visitors, some announced and some not, all deserving hospitality."

"Do all animals and farmhands on the farm bring you happiness?"

"Some do and some do not. Most do, but not all the time."

"How do you manage problems on the farm?"

"I have learned a technique I call POUT."

"How does POUT work?"

"Let me tell you a story. Some time ago, your Aunt Ethis came to the farm. We decided to prepare a meal to celebrate her visit. We went to the chicken coop to collect eggs but realized that our chickens had been lazy and had produced only one egg. We both needed the egg.

We started arguing why it was more important to each one of us to have the egg. Things got heated. We both felt angry and started calling each other names. Emotions had gotten the best of us even though we still loved and respected each other deeply.

We started blaming each other for our lack of mutual flexibility or the inability to understand each other. We each took our position and were not going to compromise as it would mean either being right or being wrong."

"So, blame got in the way?"

"Yes, blame leads straight to the bad land. It always does. We needed to not blame each other but switch to being accountable to solving the problem that was at hand, for that accountability is the

---

[1] J. Krakauer. 2007. *Into the Wild* (New York: Anchor Books), p. 189.

pillar of problem-solving and continuous improvement. This blaming and lack of accountability became known as the 'escape goat' pitfall at the farm."

"Who got the egg in the end?"

"Your Aunt Ethis and I discussed our desire to reach a win–win situation, moving from give and take to give and receive.

After a few hours of pondering, we decided to use a framework we called POUT. This framework is used by mediators and great salespeople alike. It works like this. Each letter is an acronym. With each letter there is a rule to follow."

Table 1.2.1 POUT *acronym and rules of* POUT

Acronym	Rule
P is for focus on the Problem not the Person	Write down the problem without using any personal pronouns (I, me, you, him, her, them, etc.).
O is for Options	List as many options as possible. Respond with "Yes, it is an option" when others state their options.
U is for Underlying interest	Find out what the other person really wants that is often left unspoken.
T is for Time for a Third Party	When P. O. U. have not produced a viable outcome, it is time to ask for the help of a third party.

"How did it work with the egg?"

"At first, we got sidetracked about the kinds of dishes we wanted to prepare and the sorts of wine that would pair best with each one of them. We had to focus our thoughts on defining the problem at hand. We could not use personal pronouns, which was the first rule of P.

We settled on: *"two parties need one egg for their respective recipe but there is only one egg available causing a shortage of one egg."* By stating "two parties," we had removed ourselves from the problem and kept emotions at bay in the process."

"Was that it for the P. and the rule of P?"

"Yes, it was quite simple. We then moved on to creating as many options as we possibly could. Some were silly but we did not laugh. We kept our comments to 'yes, that is an option.'"

"What were some of the options you came up with?"

"There were many. I cannot recall all of them but here are some I do:

- One party could have the egg and the other party could choose a different recipe that would not require an egg.
- Both parties could wait until later in the day to check if more eggs had been laid while speaking a few words of encouragement to the chickens.
- The celebration could be delayed by one day in the hope that more eggs would be laid with the extra time allowance.
- Both parties could run to the store and buy one egg or order a one-egg delivery to the farm.

They were all options."

"Did you and Aunt Ethis choose an option?"

"No, we moved on to the U. of POUT before selecting the option that would get us to a win–win situation.

Aunt Ethis asked me what I was going to cook that required an egg? I told her that I needed the yoke for my ganache, a chocolate filling. I asked her, in turn, what it was that she was going to make that required an egg? Aunt Ethis told me that she needed the white for her whipped cream. Knowing the underlying assumption helped us find yet another win–win option."

"So, you did not have to use the T. of POUT?"

"Correct, we were able to solve our problem with P.O.U. only. Most often than not, if you teach the POUT framework to everyone you interact with in life, you will rarely use the T. Sometimes life will place a tough nut in your hands and using the T. will help you crack it. I never hesitated to call upon your Grandma, a friend, or a counselor of any kind. Sometimes the third party is not even a person. A coin or a game of rock, paper, scissors can serve as an impartial third party."

"It sounds like POUT can be used to solve almost any problem, big or small."

"It can Granddaughter. As a matter of fact, it is so important and effective that in the courtyard of the farm, we laid down rocks to form four squares. At the intersection of the four squares we built a fountain to remind us to use this framework at every opportunity."

"So, with POUT Grandpa, all animals and farmhands end up bringing you happiness?"

"Not all animals and farmhands bring happiness Granddaughter. Some animals and farmhands will not succeed in moving past the first rule of P. We cannot change others. We can only help them change themselves if they are willing. It is up to us to find our own happiness."

CHAPTER 3

Mindfulness

"The sun is starting to heat things up and my muscles could use a bit of rest Granddaughter. How about if we let the current carry us for a few minutes as we continue this discussion."

"That sounds good to me; paddling is hard work. Is POUT the only thing you use on the farm to help with happiness Grandpa?"

"It surely helps reduce negative emotional responses and helps tackle conflicts Granddaughter, however, there are other techniques I discovered and learned from wise souls who crossed my path to get to an even better place."

"What other techniques?"

"Some years back, I created a new field on the farm and have visited it almost daily since. Sometimes I just stay there for a few minutes. Sometimes I linger for an hour or more. The more time I spend in that field, the more time I want to spend there.

From the farmhouse, I walk down the main road for two minutes, turn left, and walk for another minute. There are no fences. There, a few paces from the road, piles of ancient, graceful dolomites welcome me with their soft, sandy tones and round, eroded shapes. I find my way to the top, sometimes with ease, sometimes with pain. I sit in a comfortable yoga-like pose, straighten my body as if a thread is running through my back, exiting through the top of my head and reaching to the sky. I focus my mind on my breath, inhaling, exhaling, allowing the present and the physical world to just be as they are. Mindfulness is about being deeply aware of our place in the universe at the present time."

"How about thoughts that won't go away?"

"At first, these thoughts will be many, but with time and practice they will be less and less frequent. When sitting on the top boulder, the bad land is right behind my back. The black birds are always available to pick up a gently wrapped negative thought. As for positive thoughts, I recognize them, acknowledge them, lay the words flat in my mind's eye, and let them gently float down until they rest on the tips of the strands of grass. They will rest there waiting to be picked up once I am ready to return to the farm."

"So, every time you go to the field of mindfulness, you are successful at letting the present be?"

"More often than not, it is a struggle. Like all things we learn in life, only with years of practice will one become more proficient."

"Is there anything else that can help you let the present be?"

"The key is a healthy body and mind. Our bodies and minds are sacred and should be nourished physically, mentally, and morally with positive energy."

"Do you have to go to the field of mindfulness to practice Grandpa?"

"The field of mindfulness is only one thought away. You can practice anywhere and anytime. It is better to practice a few minutes every day rather than one hour a month. It is also more fruitful to make time for longer mindfulness sessions in a familiar place. Only after all physiological and safety needs are met are we able to fulfill our need for love, belonging, and esteem Granddaughter. Mindfulness is a tool to reach the most one can be, not only on the farm but also in our personal lives, or as Grandma calls it, self-actualization."

CHAPTER 4

Waste

"As you practice mindfulness Grandpa, do you have time for any other work on the farm?"

"Most of the time is spent working on the farm Granddaughter. Mindfulness is the work we do on ourselves."

"What other work do you do on the farm?"

"Like most farms, we work with the land and animals to create our subsistence. We started with a few head of cows and a few sheep as our guests."

"Why do you call them guests?"

"Well, the animals on my farm are free to come and go as they wish."

"I love cows and sheep. Can you 'draw me a sheep?'[2]"

"I will later tonight, Granddaughter, after we set up camp, but as you love animals so much I think you'll enjoy hearing about how we began our milking operations on the farm. We decided to do the setup in the 'O' barn next to the farmhouse. We call it the 'O' barn because it is in the shape of an 'O.' With our cows and sheep ready to get to work, we were prepared to start collecting their milk. We thought we were smart and had it all figured out. We split our cows into groups of 12. We took our first group of cows and milked them in one batch. Sure, some cows got bored as they waited and waited for their turn in a long line outside. The sheep too, complained with loud 'baaahs' as they waited for all the cows to be milked first. At times, some sheep tried to jump the line, but the cows felt their place in the farm society had been established centuries ago and they would not let the sheep change any of it.

---

[2]A. de Saint-Exupéry. 1998. *The Little Prince* (Hertfordshire: Wordsworth Editions Ltd.), p. 14.

Now keep in mind Granddaughter that milking a cow was a lengthy process. We first had to direct the cows to station number one to get their tails tied to their legs with a piece of twine. As the pieces of twine were not within easy reach, we were forced to turn and twist our backs and necks to grab a new one when needed. We then had to move the 12 cows to the milking stalls where we proceeded to milk them to the last drop.

We did not need all the milk right then thus had to store it. As we had milk from the day prior, we had to put the old milk aside so we could store the newest milk behind. We then had to move the old milk forward so we would be forced to use the old milk first.

Finally, we untied all the cows' tails in the last station and let the group of 12 loose in the prairie. We restarted the process for the next batch of 12 cows that were beginning to show signs of impatience. We kept going until all the cows had been milked. Next in line were the sheep. We repeated the same operation, except for the tying of the tails. We had never been trained for sheep milking, and did not feel that qualified, but still went ahead with it.

More than once, we mistakenly used a milk container for sheep milk that contained some cow milk. Sometimes we caught our mix-up, but most times it went unnoticed until the mixed milk made it to the cheesemaker's factory ending up in a cheese that did not turn out to be that great! Then we would hear a lot about our mix-up from the cheesemaker."

"What did you do with all the milk, old and new, that you stored?"

"To try to limit the rearranging of the old and new milk several times a day, we tried to plan how much the cheesemaker was going to need, but most of the time we either ran out of milk or had too much and it spoiled. We dreaded the time-consuming task of rearranging the old and new milk. It goes without saying that I did not have much time for mindfulness sessions. I was stressed on my own farm and knew that something had to be done before my stress led to illness."

"What did you do?"

"I talked to your Grandma and she said she knew someone that could help us, farmer Tim Woods. I called him and explained what was happening. He was a kind person and offered to come and visit where the milking operation was taking place, he called it the "Gemba." The next morning, I walked Tim to the 'O' barn. For a long time, he silently observed the

cows moving in groups, the sheep waiting for their turns, and the bal-
let of milk containers switching around. Later he asked many questions,
always curious and nonjudgmental. At the end of the day, he sat with all
the cows, sheep, and farmhands and admitted that his father had been a
humorous fellow matching every letter in his name with wastes encountered on most farms."

Table 1.4.1 TIM WOODS *acronym and waste definitions*

T is for Transport	Unnecessary movement of material, products, or information
I is for Inventory	Any work that is in process ahead of when it is actually needed
M is for Motion	Needless movement of body parts
W is for Waiting	Any delay between processes
O is for Overproduction	Making more than is immediately required
O is for Overprocessing	Adding more value to a service than what a customer expects
D is for Defects	Any aspect of the service that does not conform to customer needs
S is for Skills	Underutilizing capabilities, and delegating tasks with inadequate training

"This is what Tim Woods said next Granddaughter."

Table 1.4.2 TIM WOODS *acronym and waste examples*

T is for Transport	"We used to move our cows from station to station as well. We also had to constantly shuffle our old and new milk the same as you. Excessively moving cows, sheep, farmhands, and milk containers was transport waste. Because we had a few more cows and sheep on our farm than you do, we maintained logs to keep track of how much milk each cow and sheep had produced. When we wanted to reward our cows and sheep for good behavior and offer them a few extra hours on the prairie or extra grass, we had to transport the information from the milking log to the cow and sheep personal files. That was all *Transport* waste.
I is for Inventory	Our cows and sheep equally waited in long lines. All lines are piles of inventory. The twine to tie the cows' tails were stored in big buckets and we never knew how many were in them, thus we often ran out. That was all *Inventory* waste.
M is for Motion	As we were reaching for the twine in the buckets behind us, we also twisted our backs and necks every time we had to fetch a new piece of twine. After a while, some of the farmhands suffered from back pain and had to enroll in the "Find a Motion Less Aggravating" program. That was all *Motion* waste.

(continued)

Table 1.4.2 TIM WOODS *acronym and waste examples (continued)*

W is for Waiting	With all the waiting at every step of the way, our sheep were particularly affected as they had to patiently watch every cow being milked before them. Our cows, more individualistic than sheep, were mostly annoyed by having to wait their turn at each station. That was all *Waiting* waste.
O is for Overproduction	Because we tried to predict, with very elaborate forecasts, how much milk the cheesemaker would need, we tended to overproduce. Cheesemakers tend to stop working with farms that run out of milk. We did not realize that overproducing milk stressed our cows and sheep, nor did we realize that it was generating most of the other wastes. That was all *Overproduction* waste.
O is for Overprocessing	Anytime we moved the extra milk around we had to adjust the milk log. Moving cows and sheep in batches added many unnecessary steps and complicated the milking process. That was all *Overprocessing* waste.
D is for Defects	Moving the extra milk also meant that sometimes the worst happened. We lost track of which was the new milk and the old milk, and more often than not, it is the cheesemaker who would find out about our mix-up. That was all *Defect* waste.
S is for Skills	Some of the farmhands were good at calming the animals and preparing them for milking but never got the chance because of the backups and rushing to get everything done. That was all *Skill* waste."

"It sounds like Tim Wood's farm had the same issues as your farm Grandpa?"

"Exactly, all farms, no matter what they produce, are alike, even if farmers swear that their farms are different and unique."

"What did farmer Tim Woods do to make his farm run better and make his cows and sheep happier?"

"Well, this is what Tim told me. His farmhands, cows, and sheep discussed and agreed that something had to be done. They decided to observe every step of the milking operation and bring small improvements to target waste. They all agreed to carry out one small improvement per week and made themselves accountable to that commitment. They had learned to see waste."

"Did you learn to see waste too Grandpa?"

"We had many things to learn before we could understand all of farmer Tim's teachings. We first had to learn what quality meant."

"Why did you need to do that?"

"I will tell you that story next Granddaughter, but the first thing I did after Tim's visit was to walk to the mindfulness field and practice. That was a lot to take in; I needed a clear mind."

CHAPTER 5

QUALITY

"Do you feel rested enough Grandpa, should we get paddling again?"

"Rapids are coming around that bend Granddaughter, so tired or not, we should get ready for them."

"How do we travel through the rapids?"

"Don't worry. We will take it one stroke at a time, and I am here to guide you along. Now Granddaughter, knowing you, I am sure you are just itching to ask me another question?"

"Oh, stop teasing me Grandpa, but you are right, I do have another question. Did the farm and the milking of the cows and sheep start to work smoothly after farmer Tim's visit?"

"Even though we had been made aware of the different categories of waste Granddaughter, we were just at the beginning of our journey. We needed to understand a lot more to get to a place of harmony with our farmhands, cows, sheep, tools, and the work that had to be done."

"What else did you have to learn to get to the place of harmony?"

"We had many problems to deal with. Sometimes the milk was creamy and other times watery. More often than not, the milk conserved well for days but other times it spoiled quickly. Occasionally, the old and the new milk were mixed up by error, and other times, the cow and sheep milk ended up in the same container!

Even though we now knew about Tim Wood's secret, it did not help with the quality of our milk. We made plenty of errors along the milking operation. By the time we, or the cheesemaker, found out about them, errors had turned into defects. The further apart the errors and the defects were, the harder it was to fix. Sometimes the defect was so severe, like the mixing of the cow and sheep milk together, that we had to discard the whole batch. That surely did not help with morale.

We started paying more attention to that particular problem and succeeded in delivering either pure cow or sheep milk to our cheesemaker more consistently."

"The cheesemaker must have been quite happy Grandpa?"

"He was not. After a few deliveries, we decided to ask the cheesemaker if he needed more milk. We thought we had, after all, fixed the cow and sheep milk mix-up issue. His answer surprised us. He said that what he wanted, above all else, was more consistent creaminess of our milk, rather than more milk.

We had focused on one problem but still had many more to address. We could not possibly focus on all of them at once. This was a puzzle. The cheesemaker had taught us another important lesson; quality was not what 'we' thought of the quality of our milk, but instead it was the degree of excellence as perceived by the cheesemaker.

We then gathered our farmhands, cows, and sheep and asked them how they perceived the quality of our milk and received another big surprise. Every person or animal gave a different answer. Some said the milk was of great quality because it was not too creamy, while others said it was of poor quality because it was not creamy enough. Everyone was so confused!"

"What did you think of the quality of the milk?"

"In the end Granddaughter, it did not matter what any of us thought of the quality of the milk. What mattered most was how creamy our cheesemaker wanted our milk to be. So, all on the farm, farmhands, cows, and sheep, agreed that quality milk would be the cheesemaker's requirement of 50 percent creaminess. Then we all went to work to achieve this standard."

"Was the cheesemaker happy?"

"Now that we knew what the quality standard was for creaminess, we still had many other issues to fix to satisfy the cheesemaker and those working on the farm. The sheep were still mad at the cows as they still had to wait in line for their turn. The cows were still irritated with each other as they also had to wait for the 12 cows in front of them. Cows and sheep were jealous of the farmhands who told them what to do all the time. All the animals envied the high-performing cows and sheep as they were given more prairie time and occasionally extra grass. Even though we could see our waste, we were still organized the same way and were almost as inefficient as before. With low morale, and most cows, sheep, and farmhands thinking only about themselves, no one was interested in fixing the defects that were passed down. They just accepted them with some sizable moaning. Most were not too concerned about the defects they created and were happy to pass them along to get rid of them."

"That must have been a hard thing to fix Grandpa."

"It surely was! First, I went back to the field of mindfulness. I knew I needed to detach myself from the problem by visualizing it as its own entity floating in front of me. That way I could manipulate it and examine it under various angles. Before taking this all on, I also needed to rejuvenate my spirit. After a successful mindfulness practice, I returned to calmness and serenity. Once the problem stood separate from any person or animal, and the emotions were kept at bay, I summoned everyone on the farm and conducted POUT sessions."

"What were the options that turned up?"

"We all agreed that we had to check for defects first. It was clearly everyone's responsibility.

Our neighbor farmers Joseph and Edwards, having heard about our troubles, recommended we read the latest issue of the *Cultivators' Digest* and the featured article '*The Question of Quality and Morale.*' Based on this fresh reading, we realized that we were at Quality Level One: Our customers were the ones inspecting our milk. That was the worst we could do.

Level 1	Customer inspects

Figure 1.5.1 Level One–customer inspection

So, Granddaughter, we started inspecting the milk ourselves for mix-up and creaminess before shipping it to the cheesemaker. The article called this Level Two.

Level 2	Company inspects

Figure 1.5.2 Level Two–company inspection

After a few weeks at Level Two, we realized how much milk we were discarding. Instead of inspecting the milk right before it shipped, we asked that the farmhands inspect the result of their operation at each station of the milking process instead. According to the article this was Level Three.

Figure 1.5.3 Level Three–work unit inspection

Figure 1.5.4 Level One to Three–checking for defects

At this point, we were only checking for defects. We saw that at each station milk was still being discarded, though not as much as was observed at Level One or Level Two. We understood that we had to tackle the bull by the horns, a favorite expression of the cows on the farm. We invited Joseph and Edwards to come and talk with everyone. They told us to recognize the importance of each and every farm inhabitant regardless of where one stood on the farm's hierarchy. The whole is the sum of its parts and no less! We all had to be invested in checking for errors rather than just finding defects.

We conducted many team-building exercises with the cows, sheep, and farmhands so that everyone would get along better and learn to work as a team. There was a lot of fighting at first. The farmhands lost their tempers a few times, pounding their chests in discontent as it was a big change for them. They had to go from telling the sheep and cows what to do all the time to asking them how it should be done. They were working for the animals instead of the other way around. Almost everyone eventually found their place based on personality, likes, dislikes, wants, needs, and beliefs.

The farmhands started relying on the cows and sheep to tell them how to best do the work, and the cows and sheep had each other's back. From this point forward, we decided to start with trust rather than with mistrust.

Some cows, sheep, and farmhands had a hard time finding their place in this new way of working and had to leave the farm. Eventually, all cows, sheep, and farmhands started checking for their own errors. We had risen to Level Four."

Figure 1.5.5 Level Four–self-inspection

"At Level Four, did you still have to discard any milk due to mix-up Grandpa?"

"There were still a few times when the cows' milk was mixed with the sheep milk. After discussing the issue with the sheep, the cows, and the farmhands, we designed two hoses used for milking, each with a different diameter and color. For the green hose, one of the ends could only attach to the cows' milk container while the other end could only fit on the cows' teat. For the orange hose, one of the ends could only attach to the sheep milk container while the other end could only fit on the sheep teat. We had discovered Level Five. We had eliminated the opportunity for error. We have never had milk mix-up since and we adopted a new mantra 'Accept, Create, and Pass on no defect.'"

Levels of a Quality System

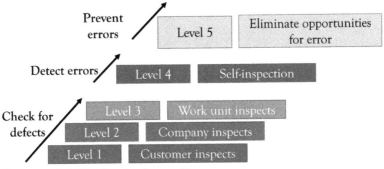

Figure 1.5.6 Five levels of a quality system

CHAPTER 6

Visual Workplace and Daily Management Systems

"You did a great job paddling through those troubled waters Granddaughter."

"I was a little scared at first and I got soaking wet, but I am happy I overcame my fear and I learned a lot about quality and morale."

"After passing through rapids, we always come out better prepared for the next ones. Let us paddle to the sandy beach around the next curve and break for lunch."

"Sounds great. I am starving. During lunch can I ask you more questions?"

"Sure thing Granddaughter."

"With everyone seeing waste, understanding what quality and the five levels were Grandpa, were all the sheep, cows, and farmhands happy?"

"They were happier than they had ever been Granddaughter, but with everyone with more skin in the game, we understood that continuous improvement was an endless journey. Pursuing quality in all we do is a mindset. It is as much about the milk and the cheese as it is about the fabric that weaves us together and connects us to our environment."

"What more was there to do?"

"Continue to learn as we kept traveling on our journey. Learning comes from unexpected times and places. After a long day in the milking barn, Grandma and I would return to the farmhouse for dinner. Frequently, other family members, animals, and farmhands would join us as we all had an equal place at the table.

To prepare for the meal, Grandma and I had a nightly ritual. One of us would open the recipe box and select one recipe card at random. We would first divide and conquer the various tasks of weighing and measuring all the ingredients on the card. We would then read the instructions out loud from start to finish for all to hear and then meticulously follow the instructions, one step at a time, cutting, mixing, layering, or whatever else was required by the recipe. We would set the oven temperature to the degree shown on the recipe card and resume our discussions while our meal was cooking. We would regularly check to make sure it was cooking evenly, and the desired outcome achieved. We knew when to start the recipe as we could easily see the time needed for the preparation and the time the dish would need to spend in the oven from the instructions on the recipe card. After making a recipe many times, everyone in the kitchen started making suggestions on how to decrease the "prep" time so we could spend more time around the table telling tales."

"How did making dinner help with the milking operation?"

"We had not yet connected all the dots. We saw that morale had greatly improved. The sheep, cows, and farmhands were proposing their weekly improvement ideas. All was going well until the day the animals and farmhands sent in their representative with one simple question: 'Are our recommendations actually improving the work and the work environment?'"

"How did you respond Grandpa?"

"The truth is that we did not know how to answer that question for 'without standards, there can be no improvement.[3]' Every day at the milk barn, we were running a marathon but never recorded our time! We gathered with the sheep, cows, and farmhands once more and came up with an idea. What we needed was a recipe card just like the one we used in our kitchen.

These work instructions would help produce quality milk, more quickly, while improving our working conditions. We set out to write step-by-step instructions for our processes. Some looked like our recipe cards, while others ended up being visual displays to make it easier to read as our hands or hooves were busy with the work. We even wrote checklists to make sure we would not miss important steps for critical processes. We marked the time it took to perform the process from the beginning to the

---

[3]van Vliet, V. 2017. "Taichi Ohno," https://www.toolshero.com/toolsheroes/taiichi-ohno/ (6/22/20).

end on top of each instruction. From that point forward, we knew if an improvement idea made a process better or worse."

"How did you measure the time it took to complete the task at each station?"

"The first idea we had was to give a stopwatch to each lead sheep or lead cow at each station so they could time how long it took to run work through their stations.

When we came back to check on progress, it was a total disaster. Lead cows were frantically trying to record all events that were happening concurrently throughout their stations. They looked panicked as they attempted to write down every start and end time. A majority of the data captured was missing either a start or a stop time. The sheep were not faring any better as they had stopped and restarted the timer so many times that the button had become stuck and would randomly pop out of the stopwatch generating bad data. It was time to take a deep breath and visit my mindfulness field for a few minutes. Hope seemed to be our last and only way out!

That is when our only bull on the farm, old and attentive to details, told us a trick he had learned on another farm in his younger days. He said that the key was to never stop the watch. 'The goal is to record the time it takes the cow to go through each station as well as the time it takes for the cow to go through every subprocess within each station. The time recorded within a station will show some wasted time between each subprocess,' old Bull added.

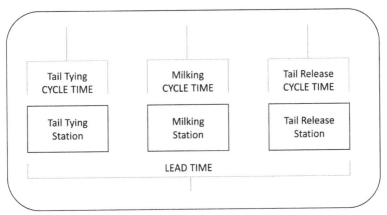

Figure 1.6.1 Lead time and cycle time

He then sheepishly said, which was odd for an old bull, that the entire time, from start to finish, including all the waiting in-between stations and in-between subprocesses was called Lead Time (LT). He added that the time it took for each individual subprocess within each station was referred to as the Cycle Time (CT).

Following the teachings of humble and wise Bull, we restarted recording time using this new method and became successful after a few supervised trials. We had gained a clear picture of all the waiting waste of the entire milking operation."

"Did capturing the time that way help with new improvements Grandpa?"

"Yes, it did. We were able to tweak our entire process flow. We were careful to simplify and not add layer upon layer of complexity. We continued to find ways to make it easier and less strenuous for the sheep, cows, and farmhands. We tried new things all the time and failure was proof that we were trying."

"With all the 'recipes' in place, were all the sheep, cows, and farmhands more productive and happier?"

"We still saw a great deal of confusion at times Granddaughter. Some sheep and cows and farmhands simply had to read a recipe one time and were able to perform their tasks well. Others had to read the recipe many times over before being successful at their duties. A few did not like to read the recipe cards and had some good days and bad days; thus, we weren't always able to predict when they would produce quality milk for the cheesemaker."

"What did you do to help all the sheep, cows, and farmhands follow the recipe and have only good days?"

"The burden was on everyone. We call it accountability. The sheep and cows were accountable to each other to be good teammates and produce quality milk every day. The farmhands were accountable to themselves by reminding the offending sheep and cows that they needed to follow the standard work to be good teammates. A few sheep, cows, and farmhands would not change their way of doing things and had to leave the farm. The secret was to make following the recipe so easy that it would take more effort to not follow it."

"What did you do to help everyone become good teammates?"

"We all decided that a board would be placed up on the wall at each station of the milking operation. Each team would huddle in front of it at eight o'clock for no more than ten minutes. The rule was that all participants had to stand. Each day the huddle would be run by a rotating team member so that all got a chance to run the huddle.

Each team working at a station of the milking process had to write its 'board statement of purpose' explaining in one short sentence the goal of its board. The cow tail tying team wrote 'The purpose of our board is to provide key indicators for our operation and a status of the improvement ideas for the tail tying team.'"

They decided to divide the board into two sections. They dedicated the first section to all the metrics and measurements to show how the tail tying operation was running. The second section was reserved for showing all the team improvement ideas and the progress made in implementing them. They referred to the first section as 'RUN THE BUSINESS' and the second section as 'IMPROVE THE BUSINESS.'

The other teams quickly adopted the two-section concept for their own boards but had different statements of purpose and metrics to match their operations. With that, we started each day with our daily team huddles with each team following its own standard agenda that was also written somewhere on the board."

"What do you mean by standard agenda Grandpa?"

"The standard agenda helped each team define the topics it wanted to cover every day. Building a standard agenda ensured that each team would not skip an important topic or start to ramble or 'baaah' or 'moo' endlessly. At first, the topic on the standard agenda changed frequently but after a few months the topics to cover became quite stable. The standard agenda for the milking station team looked like this:

- Recognition and awards
- Yesterday's metrics
- Today's objectives
- Improvement status
- New improvement ideas
- Fun fact and quiz of the day
- Word of the day."

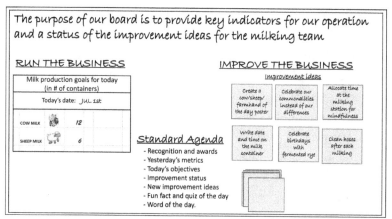

Figure 1.6.2 Visual board with run the business and improve the business sections

"We also saw value in having a milk barn huddle as this gave a venue for every team involved in the milk production to check on barnwide metrics and improvement ideas."

"With all the team huddles and the use of the boards, were all the sheep, cows, and farmhands in a happy mood Grandpa?"

"The mood of all people and animals at the farm was the best we had ever had Granddaughter, but we knew we could make it even better. It was hard work, no doubt about that. We did not know what was coming next on our journey, but we knew we would find out soon enough."

CHAPTER 7

Problem-Solving and True Deep Root Causes (TDRCs)

"Those sandwiches you packed for lunch were delicious, but the mosquitoes are eating me alive Grandpa, should we head back to the canoe?"

"We will in a few minutes. For the time being, let us look at the beauty that surrounds us. If we focus on the positive, we will soon stop noticing those little bites."

"How much further do we have to go today Grandpa?"

"In a couple of hours we will reach our campsite for the night."

"I can't wait to be around the campfire roasting marshmallows and making S'mores. In the meantime, can we keep talking about the farm Grandpa."

"Yes, back to the farm. We all thought we had made great advances in our pursuit of perfection until that one morning when a particularly vocal cow announced at the barnwide huddle in one frothy breath, 'the temperature in the milk barn along with the irregular morale of my colleagues the cows and sheep, and the fact that the windows are sometimes open and sometimes half closed, are making all our farmhands cranky, and it is their responsibility to ensure that the milk gets stored at or below the safe temperature, and that we, sheep and cows, should not be blamed for the spoiled milk, when in fact, if the farmhands did what they were supposed to do, we would not have any problems, and the farm would be the paradise we all aspire it to be!'"

"That is a bit confusing to me Grandpa! What was the problem you had to deal with this time?"

"First, I needed to travel back to the field of mindfulness to clear my thoughts and return to awareness Granddaughter. After connecting with the conspiring universe around me for a few hours, I paused and thought about the

POUT framework that your Aunt Ethis and I developed to see how it could help in this situation, but it was not enough. There was just too much information in the statement that the vocal cow had made. I was confused and lost!

That is the moment Robin Zupashas, a visitor who had recently arrived on the farm, walked toward me as I was on my way back to the barn. He approached, put a calming hand on my shoulder, and said he could help. He explained he was a founding member of the TDRCC, which stands for True Deep Root Cause Council. Root reminded me of trees, plants, and other kinds of shrubbery. I had to ask him what this had to do with our milk problem?

Robin smiled and explained that it was a common misunderstanding. He recommended that we first seek the help of the vocal cow to clearly and simply define the problem. He added that we live in a complex world in which an infinite number of moving parts affect each other and are surrounded by the dense fog of the unknown. As if that was not enough, he then delivered an even more insightful comment: '*always reframe the problem by asking what causes what by how much?*'

With that truth said, he asked us to sit down with the cows, farmhands, and sheep to work through the statement the vocal cow had made. Using our POUT skills, we knew the first thing to do was to remove the person and focus on the problem while avoiding blame. Once that was done, the statement was already easier to grasp.

Initially, we struggled, but with Robin's help we agreed on the following problem statement: '*Undocumented standards for airflow, milk storage temperature, and assignment of responsibilities cause 20 percent of the milk to spoil.*' At last we had something to work with."

"So now you knew what to do Grandpa. By fixing the airflow, controlling the milk storage temperature, and documenting who does what, you would have no more spoiled milk!"

"We still had a few more things to learn from our TDRCC visitor. Before moving on, Robin asked us to review our problem statement by asking the following questions:

- 'Does the statement address only one problem?
- Is the statement no more than two sentences?
- Are solutions suggested in the statement?

- Does the statement attribute blame?
- Does the statement contain assumptions?'

He also explained that we needed to teach our problem-solving brain to stop assuming that we know the deep root cause.

Our problem statement indicated surface root causes: the airflow, the milk storage temperature, and the responsibility assignment. We had not found the deep root cause yet as it takes effort to dig for the deepest roots of a tree.

Robin then went on to teach us a powerful tool he called the Five Whys. He said that there are many other tools in his toolbox for deep root cause investigation but the Five Whys was a powerful one to start our deep root cause exploration."

"Did you use the Five Whys with Grandma and other family members to solve problems?"

"You bet I did! All the lessons I learned at the farm served me well in all sorts of problem situations. We started applying our first Five Whys with the airflow issue. It went like this:

Why didn't we have a standard for airflow?

- Because nobody knew it affected milk spoilage.
  Why didn't anybody know that airflow affected milk storage?
- Because no one was trained on milk production environmental factors.
  Why was no one trained on milk production environmental factors?
- Because we did not have a production environmental factors training program.
  Why didn't we have a production environmental factors training program?
- Because no one was in charge of establishing a training program.

We had found our first deep root cause. We also had a second answer to the question: Why didn't anybody know that airflow affected milk storage? This led us down to a different branch of our Five Whys to look for another deep root cause.

Why didn't anybody know that airflow affected milk storage?

- Because no one was in charge of measuring airflow and its effect on milk storage.

  Why was no one in charge of measuring airflow and its effect on milk storage?

- Because we had not established a clear list of duties and responsibilities assignment.

We had found a second, deep root cause for the lack of standard airflow.

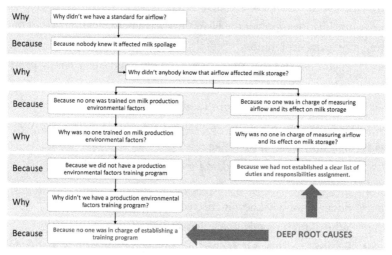

Figure 1.7.1 Five Whys root cause drill down

We repeated the exercise for the milk storage temperature and the responsibility assignment. It became much easier as we practiced the Five Whys. We found two additional deep root causes:

Because the milk storage room was not separated from other milk stations.

Because we had no system to cool the milk storage area."

"How do you know how many Whys to ask Grandpa?"

"Sometimes you get to the deep root cause by answering two Whys, sometime by answering more than Five Whys. The key is to stop when the answer becomes actionable, meaning that you can do something about it, or when the answer becomes silly."

"Did you get to some silly answers?"

"We surely did. When we asked why the milk storage room was not separated from other milk stations, one sheep stated that it was because everybody knows that at the farm there is no privacy. It is true that we were all smiles at that point, but more seriously, we realized that what we had learned was due to a dramatic change in our way of thinking. It forced us not to pick on the first thing we saw as the cause but to dig further for the deep root cause of a problem.

We had learned that without dealing with the deep root cause, the pain would come back time and time again. Acting on the surface root cause wastes energy and destroys spirits not only at the farm but all places in our lives."

"So now that you had all the deep root causes Grandpa, you could solve the spoiled milk problem for good."

"We had yet another lesson to learn. When we looked at our deep root causes, the cows, farmhands, and sheep alike felt overwhelmed by the need to tackle all of them at the same time. Once again, Robin, our TDRCC visitor, came to our rescue with yet another tool, the Interrelationship Diagram, to separate cause from effects. That was a necessary step to find the **true** deep root cause. He told us to ask the following question for each deep root cause: 'does this deep root cause produce other deep root causes?' If the answer was yes, we had to draw an arrow to indicate causality. We then counted how many times each deep root cause produced the other.

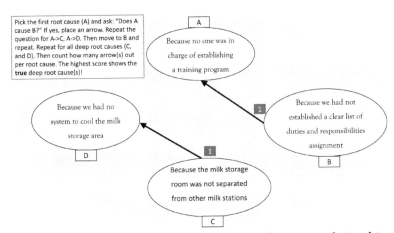

Figure 1.7.2 Separating causes and effects with an interrelationship diagram

It became clear that:

- No separate milk storage room caused the inability to build a cooling system.
- No clear assignment of responsibilities caused that no one was in charge of a training program.

Robin concluded that by working only on the very few **true** deep root causes (TDRCs), rather than their effects, we could have a sizable impact on the outcome while using limited resources. As an example, he told us that how much money the farm would make over the years was an effect of the quality of our milk, the skills of our cows, farmhands, and sheep, the morale of all involved, and a balanced and sustainable environment. These were the things that we needed to focus on to thrive over the long run. Humanity and environment would become our keys to success."

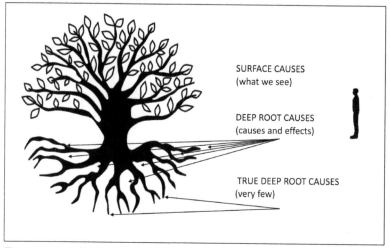

SURFACE CAUSES
(what we see)

DEEP ROOT CAUSES
(causes and effects)

TRUE DEEP ROOT CAUSES
(very few)

Figure 1.7.3 Looking for true deep root causes

CHAPTER 8

Countermeasures

"Look Granddaughter, our campsite is in sight. A few more strokes and we will break for the night. We are halfway through our trip. Most importantly, do you know what comes after hard work?"

"Would it be S'mores Grandpa?"

"S'mores over a wood fire under the stars is right! We can set up camp and then keep chatting."

"OK. So, I am wondering Grandpa, by finding the TDRCs, were you able to stop getting spoiled milk?"

"With our TDRCs uncovered Granddaughter, we all set out to take care of them. We were TDRC hunters!

The curliest sheep of our flock said he would take on the "storage room not built separately" and the cow with a brown spot shaped like the state of Alaska on her flank said she would address the "no clear responsibilities assignment." The farmhands cheered and asked if there was anything they could do to help support the effort. The cows and sheep acknowledged the offer and responded that if the need arose, they would take them up on their offer.

The next few days the milk production steadily increased as large orders from the cheesemaker came in. The milk barn was a busy place with the teams huddling and checking their progress, and team members looking for new improvement ideas to put on the board.

A few more weeks passed. We looked at the barn and saw no signs of construction around the milk storage area. We asked around to find out if anyone knew about any construction plans and received blank stares in response. We went to look for Curly sheep first and learned that she had been placed in quarantine after a particularly severe episode of anxiety that had caused her fleece to go totally straight. We felt sorry for what had happened. We next went to check on Alaska's progress on her work to address the TDRC of no clear responsibilities assignment. She explained that she got really busy with the additional milk demand, had other priorities, and was too busy to talk with us any longer. She looked so stressed that her trademark tattoo now looked more like the continent of Antarctica! We questioned the farmhands who told us they had lost track of time as they were concentrating on prepping the next team potluck to improve low morale. What a disappointment it was!"

"Did you ask more serious and committed sheep, farmhands, and cows to take on the TDRCs?"

"No blame, no blame … the method that we had used to tackle the TDRCs was the faulty part. We also realized we had another significant failure on our hands and hooves. We had forgotten to teach our sheep, farmhands, and cows how to build their own farm in the sky. They too needed to have their bad land, black birds, and fields of mindfulness. Only if all of us on the farm were to practice mindfulness could we detach from the past, stop projecting ourselves in the future, and fully focus on what was happening right at the moment, in the present. So, before resuming our journey, we pressed the pause button and trained everyone on the farm.

Overworking sheep, farmhands, and cows is one of the worst things one can do on a farm.

Working smarter, not harder was an important lesson learned. We provided time in the day for retreats to the field of mindfulness when things got tense. We also added a new metric on the *Improve the Business* side of the board where once a week each team member wrote an 'S' if they were satisfied with their mindfulness practice or a WOI if they were 'Working On It.'

As for the faulty method we had used with Curly (now temporarily referred to as Straight-Fleece) and Alaska (momentarily Miss Antarctica), we learned our next lesson from a little lamb, wooly and smart. She told us that when she wanted a new chewy toy 'really baaahdly,' she would simply ask her parents to go to the store and buy the toy while it was on sale. Hearing that statement, a farmhand said that this resembled some technique he had witnessed on another farm that translated into WHAT? BY WHOM? BY WHEN? The farmhand also told us that the "WHAT" was called countermeasures at that other farm."

"So how did you work out your countermeasures for the two TDRCs?"

"After teaching all sheep, farmhands, and cows what we had just learned, we all developed our countermeasures for our TDRCs. It looked something like this:

Table 1.8.1 *Countermeasures for storage room not built separately true deep root cause*

True deep root cause	What	BY WHOM	BY WHEN
Storage room not built separately	• Draw plans for temperature-controlled milk storage room	Curly[a]	Jul 30th
	• Contract with specialized construction company	Grandma	Aug 15th
	• Build room per plan	Contractor	Sept 15th
	• Accept/Reject delivery	Milk Storage Team	Oct 15th

[a] With her new knowledge and her field of mindfulness, Curly's stress level had decreased and her curls had returned.

Table 1.8.2 *Countermeasures for no clear responsibilities assignment true deep root cause*

True deep root cause	What	BY WHOM	BY WHEN
No clear responsibilities assignment	• Inventory all major responsibilities by function	Alaska	Aug 15th
	• Assign one cow, sheep, or farmhand to each responsibility	Grandpa	Sept 15th
	• Communicate assigned responsibilities to each team member	Alaska	Sept 20th
	• Post the responsibility matrix on each team's huddle board	Alaska	Sept 20th
	• Establish and schedule a periodic review and retraining on the responsibility matrix	Grandma	Sept 20th

At each huddle we looked at our countermeasures posted on the *Improve the Business* side of our barnwide visual board. When getting to that agenda item, we asked Curly and Alaska to mark the progress they had made for each WHAT on the plan and if they needed help from anyone. We updated the board daily. It worked great!"

"How did you know that the TDRCs had been eliminated? Don't sheep, farmhands, and cows sometimes pick the wrong TDRC Grandpa?"

"We needed to continue checking the results of our countermeasures to ensure the TDRCs had indeed been eliminated. We added a new metric on the *Run the Business* side of the barnwide huddle board called Weekly Milk Spoilage. Every week we carefully monitored our milk spoilage. We then knew if our countermeasures were really working or if we needed to go back to the drawing board and rework our true deep root cause analysis. Robin congratulated us and told us that we had discovered the virtue of the PDCAS cycle: Plan, Do, Check, Adjust, Standardize. Since it was a cycle, we understood that we had to keep working through it, time and time again. He also added that after confirming the TDRCs had been eliminated, we should make our changes permanent by Standardizing the new way of working. This took us full circle through the PDCAS cycle."

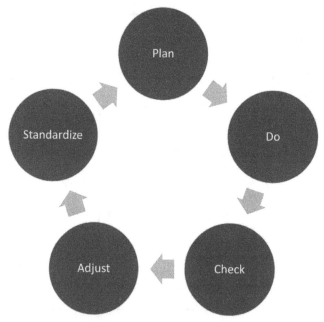

Figure 1.8.1 PDCAS plan-do-check-adjust-standardize cycle

"So, any new milk barn would have a separate temperature-controlled storage room and a clear list of assigned responsibilities, Grandpa?"

"That is correct. Every new milk barn and operations would have a set of documented policies, procedures, and detailed work instructions to follow. Some would be written on paper, some would be short films or audios, some would even be sung by the cows, sheep, or farmhands.

With all that said, it is time to hit the hay and wish you a good night Granddaughter, filled with sweet dreams in color and flying butterflies."

CHAPTER 9

Theory of Constraints (TOC)

"Did you have a good night Granddaughter?"

"No butterflies in my dreams Grandpa but lots of cows and sheep to help me get to sleep."

"That is good to hear. We should pack up our gear now and head downriver while the morning freshness lasts. I am rejuvenated and ready for your deluge of questions."

"Oh Grandpa, that is what I love so much about you. You never tire of all my questions. So, with all the work and learning at the farm, were the cows, sheep, and farmhands now happy?"

"To be happy, we must be aware of our own well-being and of all the good as it is happening, in the present.

It is true, Granddaughter, that we had taught everyone on the farm to attempt to live in the present through the field of mindfulness. That alone was not enough. To achieve a harmonious workplace, the cows, sheep, and farmhands also had to recognize that everyone on the farm, from the barn sweeper to the barn manager, were equal.

We all agreed that the closer to the work the better placed we were in bringing continuous improvements to our workplace. All had a stake in bringing humanity to the farm. We had learned so many things together. Besides mindfulness, we were now resolving conflicts and solving problems with the POUT framework. We were seeing and eliminating waste guided by Tim Woods. We were understanding what quality truly was from the eye of the cheesemaker. We had become a team with our huddles and were keeping a pulse on the business and monitoring our continuous improvements with our visual boards. We were digging up TDRCs and eliminating them with structured countermeasures. That WAS a lot!

Despite harnessing all these skills and frameworks, we continued to experience bouts of low morale. Sheep were still upset that they had to wait to be milked until after the cows. Most cows and sheep were particularly annoyed by some out-of-line behaviors by their peers. For instance, one of the cows, Flaky, was so concerned about cleanliness that she began putting a cap on her head as she entered each station and removing it as she left. The entire milk production would painfully slow down to match Flaky's own rhythm. Some sheep and farmhands were equally responsible for slowing down the milk barn operations. One sheep, for example, was spending a lot of time gathering and spreading gossip. Even some of the farmhands were excelling at gathering data endlessly, unfortunately, without making any use of it. We could only go as fast as the slowest of our participants. Even Vocal Cow had no statements to make on how to ease our pain!"

"How did you get out of that tough pickle?"

"We were ready to learn our next lesson. Our fluffiest cat on the farm, EliGo, had been observing our struggle. He revealed that among his many talents he was also a Catsultant ready to provide advice. He added, to entice us, that he had seen a lot in his 15 cat years and that he knew exactly how to deal with our slow rhythm and bottlenecks. He told us that a framework, referred to as Theory of Constraints (TOC) was the tool to use for such situations and that he would spare his knowledge for a few extra portions of wet cat food and a bag of catnip. After we agreed to his shameless demands, he stated that the TOC applies to every system that surrounds us, whether in the milk barn, on the farm, or in our personal lives. The first step was to identify the constraint or bottleneck.

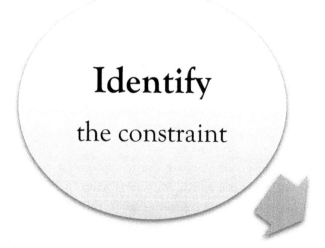

Figure 1.9.1 Identify the constraint

We decided to focus on Flaky's issue first as she was one of our bottlenecks. EliGo told us that the second step was to exploit the constraint, which meant reducing the bottleneck while using only available resources.

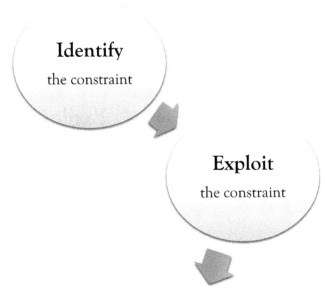

Identify

the constraint

Exploit

the constraint

Figure 1.9.2 Exploit the constraint

To fulfill the requirements of this step, we asked Flaky to shampoo her hair every morning with a specially formulated shampoo we had available on the farm."

"Did it work Grandpa?"

"It really helped. After a few days, Flaky gained confidence in herself and her scalp and put a cap on her head only as she entered the milk barn, removing it only when she left the barn to return to pasture. We saw Flaky move a lot faster through every station as she did not have to stop at each station to change her cap anymore. As Tim Woods had taught us, we had eliminated a lot of extra motion and overprocessing.

To learn about the third step EliGo told us it would cost us two extra bags of catnip and one Copper River salmon as we had run out of the hours allocated for his intervention. We were eager to learn more and had to pony up the extra catnip and the fish. He went on to explain that the third step was to subordinate and synchronize all processes to our constraint.

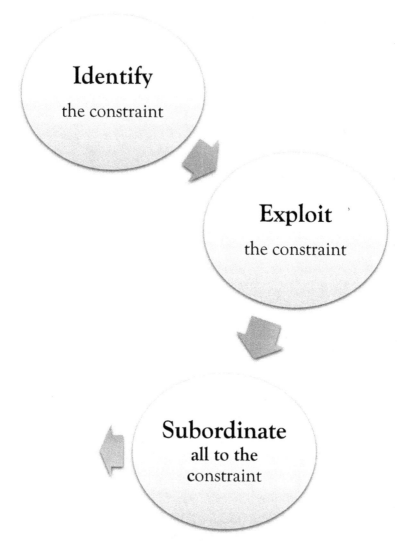

Figure 1.9.3   Subordinate all to the constraint

This meant that all the stations had to run at the same pace as Flaky's, no faster and no slower. Running any faster would only create inventories of milk, cows, and sheep for the stations upstream while causing lots of waiting and idle time for the stations downstream. After adjusting the upstream and downstream stations to match Flaky's pace, EliGo asked us to verify if Flaky was still the constraint as it is common for the constraint to move somewhere else. Flaky was still the slowest cow in the entire barn. As a result, EliGo instructed us to move to step four of the TOC method, elevate the constraint.

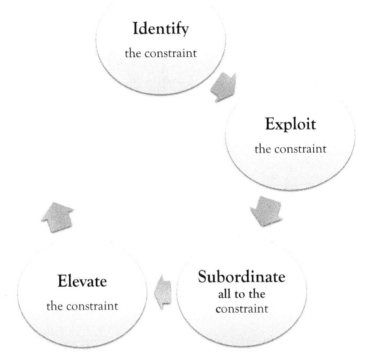

Figure 1.9.4 Elevate the constraint

At this point we could invest additional resources to exploit the constraint further. This is what EliGo meant by "elevating." After conducting another POUT session with the cows, sheep, and farmhands, we settled on engaging the services of a dermatologist with large mammal post-doc experience. Flaky's head was initially treated daily with a special hydrating ointment. The treatment was then tapered to one application monthly as the flakes were no longer present. The treatment worked wonders. Flaky was less stressed than ever. Her worries vanished along with the need to wear her haircap. Stations upstream from where Flaky was standing started processing cows and milk faster, and stations downstream had enough work to proceed at a faster pace. EliGo praised us for making it through the first four steps and told us that one more step was necessary, repeat. At this stage in our journey this was already something quite familiar to us.

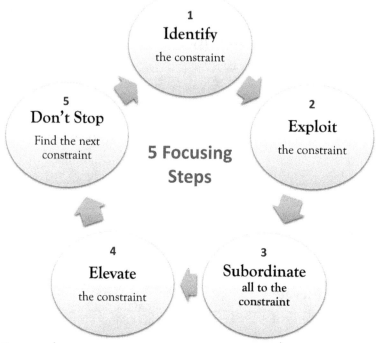

Figure 1.9.5 Find the next constraint and repeat

So you see, the pursuit of perfection never ends Granddaughter. We knew we had other constraints or bottlenecks to address and we were ready to start going through the five TOC steps again. We added this framework to the *Improve the Business* side of our visual board, taught everyone on the farm about the EliGo TOC framework, added the training to our course library for all new cows, sheep, and farmhands, and scheduled everyone for refresher training and TOC workshops every few months."

"With the EliGo TOC tool Grandpa, was the farm finally the best it could be for its inhabitants and their environment?"

"One can always do better. We should strive to learn more, for the day we stop learning is the day we stop living. We need to stay curious, and like children keep experimenting with an open mind. With that mindset, we were ready for another important lesson. One that would take us much further on our continuous improvement journey."

CHAPTER 10

Flow

"With all that talking Granddaughter, we seem to have missed our midday spot!"

"What are we going to do now?"

"As in life, at each intersection there are many paths that open up. We need to pay attention and we will see the signs. If you would like, we can practice some mindfulness together while waiting for a good omen or two."

"OK, mindfulness first and talk about the farm later?"

"That sounds like a great plan. Now let us be quiet for a few minutes and be aware of the present."

"I feel so much more alive after this practice but now my stomach is growling."

"As predicted, we paid attention, and voila, the perfect shady beach on the river revealed itself to us. Let us paddle to shore and we can resume the story while indulging in Grandma's tasty potato salad.

Our milk production business had become more complicated, Granddaughter, as new cheesemakers, having heard about the great quality of our milk had joined the ranks of our customers. Some cheesemakers were asking for skim milk, some for 20 percent fat milk, some for whole milk, and others for anything in-between. This was true for both our cow and sheep milk.

We were now running all our individual team huddles as well as the milk barn huddles; we used our visual boards efficiently with an eye on our key metrics and on the many improvements that were underway. We also had every cow, sheep, and farmhand on a daily training schedule with everyone tasked to teach each concept to each other and to new heads on the farm. It was very efficient in keeping everyone engaged and fresh on each concept. Everyone was a teacher and an advocate. We all agreed to follow this successful approach religiously.

Yet, with all the lessons learned to date we were still struggling to predict the demand for all the different sorts of milk we had to produce for the growing number of cheesemakers. It was a nightmare to keep it all together. We were experiencing high inventory levels when we miscalculated our demand forecast. We also had a lot of milk spoilage as some of the specialty milk was not following a predictable pattern and we had to discard it after a few days when not ordered.

We had wrongly gained confidence in having our days and weeks set as clockwork. Once a week all supervisors would get together with our two forecaster dogs, 'Batch' and 'Q,' and would look at how much milk each cheesemaker had ordered in the last 12 months. Some were ordering small quantities very often, and others large quantities not all that often. 'Batch' and 'Q' would retreat to the doghouse and plot the numbers on a gigantic grid. Once ready, they would add a little more to each number for good measure.

Both dogs were also tasked, to their delight, with rounding up the lead cows and sheep every morning in the pasture to paw out their day's forecast. We would always hear quite a few 'baaahs' and 'moos' of disagreement and a few disparaging comments about how much nonsense went into the numbers. Farmhands pretended not to hear any of it and instead waited in the milk barn for the cows and sheep to arrive. Farmhands would look at the cows' daily forecast and sort by quantity, largest to smallest. They would then start with the largest quantity on the list and move the cows through each station until the desired quantity was obtained and stored (now in a nicely temperature-controlled storage room). Farmhands would proceed to the next largest quantity on the forecast and start over with a new set of cows."

"What about the sheep Grandpa?"

"Unfortunately, the sheep had to wait, often showing signs of impatience as they were uncomfortable and needed to be milked. They were not amused, Granddaughter, not amused! After all the cows had been milked, the sheep got their turn. The farmhands would start the process all over by taking the largest quantity on the list and moving the sheep through each station until the desired quantity was obtained and stored. Often the specialty milk, near the bottom of the sorted forecast, did not get processed until late in the night forcing sheep and farmhands to work overtime. Once all the quantities forecasted had been processed, customer orders could be prepared for shipping. Since the forecasted quantities were always wrong, some cheesemakers would not get all the milk they had ordered, while some milk would spoil due to lack of orders."

"That sounds like a tough problem to fix Grandpa?"

"It was Granddaughter, but fortunately, high in the rafters of the milk barn, turtle doves had been witnessing our daily struggle. We frequently heard them purr back and forth as the day went by. We reached up to them and they were quick to tell us, which was remarkable for turtle doves, that a farm where they had previously roosted had found a way to put an end to the ridiculousness of the situation. That certainly got everybody's attention!

We all gathered at a large table. We brought some seeds, hay, and dry nuts as it is never good to work on an empty stomach. Once we were properly snacked, we were ready to listen to what the turtle doves had observed.

The turtle doves told us that the milk flows much better when the layout of a barn is in a 'V' shape with a conveyor belt that follows the pattern from the entry door of the milk barn to the exit door. The cows and sheep enter the barn riding on the conveyor belt which moves them through each station. At each station, the farmhands are the ones attending to the passing cows and sheep. For example, they purred, the farmhand tasked with tail tying goes to the cow as it enters the tail tying station and ties the tail before the cow is conveyed to the next station. That station skips the sheep as sheep do not like anyone messing with their tails. When the cows and sheep enter the station downstream, a farmhand is ready to tend to them as they are passing through. This process repeats for every station. Cows and sheep are fed their daily rations of hay as they move along the milk barn keeping them satiated and calm.

Hearing that story, we heard loud 'baaahs' and 'moos' of approval and the farmhands smiled and nodded in agreement. The turtle doves explained that the farm where they had previously lived called this organization of the milk barn the One-Piece Flow."

"Did you change the layout of the milk barn to a 'V' shape with the slow-moving conveyor belt Grandpa?"

"Yes, we did Granddaughter, and we were ready to try out our new milking system in the milk barn!"

CHAPTER 11

Pull versus Push

"Are we almost there Grandpa?"

"We are getting closer, but we should finish lunch and head back to the water if we want to make it to our final destination before nightfall. As soon as we are back to paddling, I will tell you what happened next."

"I would love to hear more about the turtle doves."

"You are in luck. I can tell you that the turtle doves warned us that we had one more concept yet to learn before setting everything in motion.

They told us that we really needed to move away from the 'Batch' and 'Q' forecasts. Reading the concerns on our faces, they explained that 'Batch' and 'Q' were smart dogs and that they could easily be taught new tricks. We asked 'Batch' and 'Q' to leave their fear of power loss at the doghouse door. 'Batch' and 'Q' told us that they had a confession to make. The giant grid in the doghouse had become so complicated that they started having cold sweats and nightmares just thinking about the next forecast. They were ready to add more value to the farm by adapting to a new system.

We then asked the turtle doves if they had witnessed how the One-Piece Flow farm handled production planning. After asking for a few more seeds and some clear water, the turtle doves went on to explain that little detailed forecasting was done at the One-Piece Flow farm. Looking at a year's worth of data, the farmer, farmhands, and animals had figured out the daily demand for certain milks such as the most popular whole milk or 2 percent fat milk. These never dropped below a certain level.

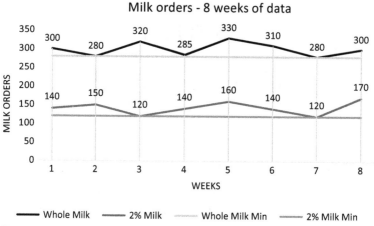

Figure 1.11.1 Milk orders by milk type

So, for these staple milks, they decided to always maintain the minimum daily quantity required in the storage room.

The One-Piece Flow farm also had small cards in the storage room that would be sent back to the lead of the first station in the milk barn anytime the quantity fell below the minimum level. The team lead would immediately pull a cow or sheep from the pasture and get her riding on the conveyor belt to replenish the staple milk above the minimum inventory level. The One-Piece Flow farm called this the *Replenishment Pull System*. The cards that were sent upstream were called KANBAN. Using this system, the farm was always able to fill any orders for staple milk, and these orders did not have to wait to be processed."

"What about the specialty milk Grandpa? What did the One-Piece Flow farm do for those?"

"Well Granddaughter, the turtle doves went on to tell us, after pecking a few more seeds, that the One-Piece Flow farm did not store any specialty milk in the refrigerated storage room. Instead, when a cheesemaker sent a specialty milk order, a new KANBAN card would be sent to the first station lead indicating exactly how much specialty milk was needed. The first station team lead would call a couple of cows or sheep from the pasture and place them on the conveyor belt to get the milking of the specialty milk started. Once the specialty milk was obtained, it would be shipped directly to the cheesemaker bypassing the storage room. The One-Piece Flow farm referred to this system as the *Sequential Pull System*.

Hearing that changeover between cows and sheep would finally be allowed generated three cheers from the sheep. On the other hoof, the cows were not pleased with the news. The turtle doves said the cows at the One-Piece Flow farm had to learn that the new way of doing things was more just and equal for everyone.

The turtle doves stated that in this system, all specialty milks were produced only when they received a specialty milk order from the cheesemaker. As the One-Piece Flow farm had used both systems, the *Replenishment Pull System* and the *Sequential Pull System*, they referred to their system as a *Mixed Pull System*."

"Why is it important for your farm to know all three Pull systems?"

"Some of the new products we would eventually add on the farm, like butter and eggs, would use a mix and match of the three Pull systems. Once again, we taught everyone on the farm about the One-Piece Flow and the Pull systems, making it part of our standard training."

"Were the farmhands, cows, and sheep happy Grandpa?"

"Happier than ever Granddaughter. We all knew, however, that the continuous improvement journey would never end."

CHAPTER 12

Change

"Can we let ourselves float again for a while Grandpa?"

"I certainly could use a little break. We have been a great team on this canoe trip. I so very much enjoy your insatiable curiosity."

"Didn't the cows, sheep, and farmhands feel overwhelmed by all the changes and learnings over time Grandpa?"

"It is true Granddaughter that we had gone through a lot together! We all struggled, at first, with so many new ways of thinking and doing. Uncertainty that comes with change had us all dreading these very changes. As we were discovering the value of doing things differently and thinking differently, little by little we became active participants embracing change. Together we had traveled as learners.

Looking back, I started the farm with a fertile field and a bad land. Then your Aunt Ethis came to visit and we devised, and used successfully, the POUT framework as a way to solve problems and conflicts. Shortly after, I discovered the importance of the field of mindfulness. At this point in my journey, animals and farmhands started arriving on the farm and learning the different categories of waste with our visitor Tim Woods. After Tim's departure, we learned what quality was from the eye of our customer, along with the five levels of quality. We were then ready to explore the use of visual management and developed our daily management system with the help of old and wise Bull. The visit from Robin, the founding member of the True Deep Root Cause Council, taught us how to problem solve more effectively, and Curly and Alaska showed us how to build effective countermeasures. Our infamous EliGo Catsultant took our learnings to the next level by helping us discover the Theory of Constraints. It is then that the turtle doves came to our rescue and told us about Flow and Pull."

"That was a lot to take in Grandpa."

"It surely was, and to answer your question, I asked EliGo if he had any insight into how we had been so successful in navigating through all that change. He said that we had indeed, unknowingly, followed a famous change framework.[4] Every time we needed to go to the next level, we were in a state of emergency. Either morale was at its lowest, cheesemakers were upset with us, the quality of milk was substandard, or our milk spoilage was through the roof. The first step in successful change, said EliGo, was to 'Create a Sense of Urgency.'

> **1- Create a Sense of Urgency**

Figure 1.12.1 Create a sense of urgency

After we accepted that we were going through a crisis, we always came together as a team to attempt to figure out a solution. EliGo stated that our behavior was in line with the second step 'Form a Powerful Coalition.'

> **2- Form a Powerful Coalition**
>
> **1- Create a Sense of Urgency**

Figure 1.12.2 Form a powerful coalition

We then brainstormed for options or engaged the help of a third party, sometimes costing us extra catnip, feed, or breadcrumbs, to help us see what the future would look like if we were to do things differently at the farm. That, Mr. EliGo said, ignoring the comments about the extra catnip, was our third step in the framework, 'Create a Vision for Change.'

Figure 1.12.3 Create a vision for change and climate for change

---

[4]Based on the Kotter Model: 8 steps for Implementing Change.

We then made sure to share our findings with the entire team. The fourth step, EliGo said, was just that: 'Communicate the Vision.'

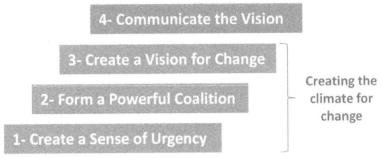

Figure 1.12.4 *Communicate the vision*

Everyone on the farm was taught that the best improvement opportunities come from those closest to the work. All felt empowered to try new things. EliGo joyously congratulated us in accomplishing the fifth step, 'Empower Action.'

Figure 1.12.5 *Empower action*

One area we could improve on, EliGo said, was the sixth step, 'Create Quick Wins.' He recommended that we advertise all the successes as they were happening on our visual boards and celebrate them at the huddles. This, he stated, would keep everyone motivated to go across the finish line.

Figure 1.12.6 Create quick wins, and engaging and enabling the organization

We knew that we did not want to return to a state of crisis after implementing a big change. Everyone on the farm had skin in the game, maybe the sheep and cows a bit more than anyone, and we all supported engraving the new way of doing things in our documentation and trainings. EliGo, once again, put his paws together and softly applauded. We had readied ourselves for steps seven and eight on the change framework: 'Build on the Change' and 'Make It Stick.'"

Figure 1.12.7 Build on the change, make it stick, and implementing and sustaining change

"With this great change framework under your belt Grandpa, were there also other nuggets that you learned for successful change?"

"Yes, Granddaughter, a few more. The most important was that we had to change the way we thought.

We had to see and keep seeing value in the new way of doing things. We realized that not until the old way was forgotten would change stick for good.

Some of us needed extra motivation at times; for that, we had to develop leadership traits in everyone to deliver on the agreed upon vision. More and more we saw sheep congratulating one another on a job well done. We also witnessed cows, sheep, and farmhands recognizing each other at the daily huddles for leading successful improvement initiatives. This boosted self-esteem and led to a sense of belonging.

It is true that at times we recognized unproductive behavior and called it out publicly for what it was, though with no blaming and no shaming in the manner it was delivered. It was important to remind everyone what the norms and values of our team were. We even encouraged laughing at our awkward selves through satire but never accepted cynicism, for cynicism is a call to passive-aggressive inaction and team demoralization. Some could not adapt to this culture and ended up leaving the farm. For all of us who decided to stay on the farm and embrace this new culture, two objectives were set: transform liabilities into assets and find joy in all we do."

CHAPTER 13

Journey

"All our paddling and drifting is paying off Granddaughter. The farm is in sight, one long straight line and we are there."

"I wish we had another day or two on the water Grandpa. I see now that many of the lessons you learned on the farm are lessons I can use in life. I am still curious about a few things though. Do we have time for a few more questions?"

"We can allow ourselves to float a little longer. I am getting older and our time together is precious. Soon enough this canoe will be yours to steer."

"With the continuous improvement philosophy in place Grandpa, what will happen to the farm and all its inhabitants?"

"When something finishes Granddaughter, it can either be seen as the end, or as the beginning of something new. Our discoveries at the farm are an ever-enriching journey as life is an endless learning pathway. It is always more about the journey than the destination."

"Was the farm complete with all its fields and buildings in place?"

"The farm is and always will be evolving. As we were learning how to best run the farm, fields and gardens were added throughout the years. All people building their farms can add the fields that feed their souls."

"What are some of the fields and gardens that you added?"

"Closest to the farmhouse, I first added the Garden of Family when I married your Grandmother. For me, this is a place of happiness and belonging as our family is what makes us whole. I added the Field of Friendship next to the Garden of Family. Flowers are cultivated in this field, some annuals, and some perennials. We never know which flowers are which when we first seed them. Next to this field, you will find the Field of Nature. This field occupies a large area of the farm. It is made up of plains, hills, forests, and deserts; many untamed animals roam its beauty. Above the hills, are mountains, complete with glaciers and summit tops. The Field of Nature is bordered on one side by an ocean and sailing vessels. I often visit the Field of Nature as it fulfills my body and nourishes my soul with the positive energy of the universe. Another field that was added is the Field of Travel. It is an ever-expanding land in which many cultures and beliefs coexist. This field is an eternal reminder of our diversity and of what unites us. In that field I often see an old man, smiling as he watches younger generations of different races and cultures, marveling at the many more years of love ahead as he contemplates his own mortality.

"Remember when I told you that Grandma said you were wise?"

"I do remember very well, and my response is unchanged; wise is what wise does. Wisdom comes with finding who we are, not who we think we want to be, building on our strengths and accepting our weaknesses. Continuous improvement applies not only to the farm and its inhabitants but also to ourselves. We must let go of our grudges and focus on the positive in everything. It is a lofty objective to attempt to become a better human being. Finding our personal mission and vision will get us closer to fulfilment and spiritual enrichment. 'All that is precious is also as difficult as it is rare.'[5]"

"I am starting to understand that the more I know about the farm, the more there is to learn. There is one mystery, that you helped me solve during our canoe trip Grandpa, and that is the meaning of the carved words on the barn door."

"Yes, Granddaughter, you are unmistakably talking about the 'THE BARN DOOR COMMANDMENTS':

Thou shall use POUT to resolve conflicts and problem solve
Thou shall not blame
Thou shall visit the mindfulness field often
Thou shall find joy in all you do
Thou shall see waste in all you do
Thou shall use effortless visual management to monitor key metrics
Thou shall relentlessly dig for the True Deep Root Cause
Thou shall use structured plans for countermeasures
Thou shall practice the PDCAS cycle for continuous improvement
Thou shall look for and address constraints
Thou shall use optimized FLOW and PULL
Thou shall use the CHANGE framework
Thou shall make everyone a teacher of LEAN."

[5] F. Lenoir. 2017. *Le Miracle Spinoza: Une Philosophie pour Éclairer Notre Vie* (Paris: Fayard), p. 248.

PART 2

The Toolshed by the Barn

"Now that we have unloaded all our gear on the pier, are we leaving the canoe in the water?"

"From this point forward, it will be for you to take out on your own journey. Let us carry it over to the toolshed to protect it from the weather while it sits idle."

"Oh my, Grandpa, this place is huge. There are so many tools in here! Look at this one, and that one over there. Have you used all of them on the farm?"

"We have used them all at one time or another Granddaughter. All the tools and frameworks in this toolshed are destined to be shared by everyone on the farm: farmhands, cows, and sheep; however, the toolshed does not hold all the tools of the universe. Its contents can, and will, be expanded as new tools show value in helping with the inner workings of the farm. Learning how to use the many tools and frameworks comes with practice though. On the farm, all the teams practice the tools on a weekly basis as no one becomes a champion in a day. Continuous improvement applies to learning too."

"How did you collect all these tools Grandpa?"

"Throughout the years, many visitors, farmhands, and animals introduced tools and methods that helped us on our infinite quest for perfection. Tools are like black boxes, input goes in one end, magic happens on the inside, and output comes out the other end. My favorite tools are the ones that are the simplest to use, with powerful alchemy on the inside, and reduced complexity in the output. We have come to categorize these tools and frameworks on the farm. The first category we call 'Whole Milk.' It groups the tools that are used the most often and work in many settings. The second category encompasses tools that are used more seldom but are useful in particular situations. We refer to this category as 'Skim Milk.' Finally, the third category, known on the farm as 'Milkshake,' combines tools into methods. To teach the tools we favored the following approach: learn two or three tools in one setting, bring two examples for each tool within 15 days, and review these examples at the team huddle."

"Can we start with the 'Whole Milk' tools Grandpa?"

"Sure thing Granddaughter, sure thing, it might take us a bit of time. Let us have a seat on these hay bales and dive in."

Whole Milk Category

Tool/Framework 1 - POUT

See Chapter 2 – POUT.

Tool/Framework 2 - Five Whys

See Chapter 7 – Problem-Solving and True Deep Root Causes (TDRCs).

Tool/Framework 3 - Interrelationship Diagram or Digraph

See Chapter 7 – Problem-Solving and True Deep Root Causes (TDRCs).

Tool/Framework 4 - Affinity Diagram

"This tool is used to reduce complexity and sort and categorize input into more useful output. It is one of my favorites, Granddaughter. In the example below, we decided to focus on our issue of *improving low morale*. We had everyone brainstorm on how to accomplish such a feat by writing down each idea on a small piece of paper. Once we were done, all the ideas looked something like this:

Table 2.4.1 Ideas generated through brainstorming

Celebrate birthdays	Set temperature in the barn higher	Exercise room
Provide bonuses	Live by the farm's values	More salt
Have monthly potlucks	More natural light	Play smooth jazz during milking
Put joke of the day on visual board	Have access to a counselor	Game room
Provide mediation services	Free treats	Pool or pond time
Treat each other with respect	More massages	Teach each other POUT
More room between milking station	Set up a hydrotherapy station	Monthly hoedown
Eat cake more often	Set temperature in the barn lower	Less shearing
Have themed lunches	Have costume contest	More green colors in the barn
Dress up for special celebrations	Be positive	Realize that we are all empowered
More whispering, less shouting	Just be good and kind animals	Bring in motivational speaker
Stop excessive mooing or baaaing	Cleaner stalls	Live in the present
More support from the farmhands	Find joy in all we do	Quiet room
Stop whining	More joy, less complaining	Animal of the month
Taco Tuesday!	Free tea, coffee, and chocolate milk	More storytelling
More brushing	Beer fridge	Stronger coffee
Less red colors in the barn	More petting	Think positively

That was a lot to digest and here is what we did next. We took the pieces of paper and randomly laid them out on a large table in the barn. We then asked every team for a volunteer to come and group *like-ideas together*. Some ideas could fit under multiple categories depending on the way they were interpreted; but in the end, it did not have to be perfect. One idea stood alone, not fitting under any of the categories and that was fine with us. After the grouping was done, we asked the team members to name each category. These are the results."

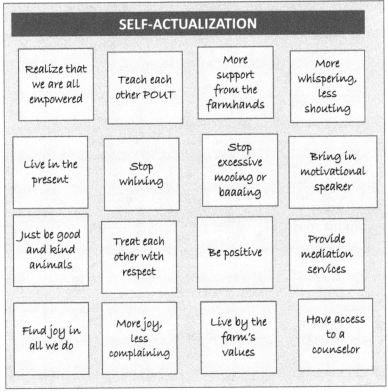

SELF-ACTUALIZATION

Realize that we are all empowered	Teach each other POUT	More support from the farmhands	More whispering, less shouting
Live in the present	Stop whining	Stop excessive mooing or baaaing	Bring in motivational speaker
Just be good and kind animals	Treat each other with respect	Be positive	Provide mediation services
Find joy in all we do	More joy, less complaining	Live by the farm's values	Have access to a counselor

Figure 2.4.1 Ideas under self-actualization category

Figure 2.4.2 Ideas under physical environment category

Figure 2.4.3 Ideas under incentives category

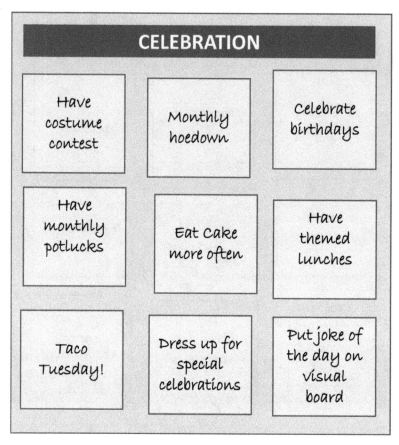

Figure 2.4.4 Ideas under celebration category

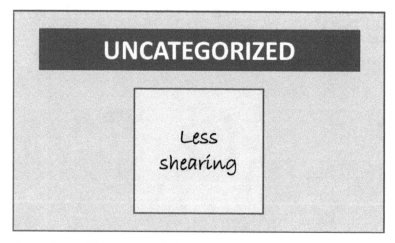

Figure 2.4.5 Uncategorized idea

The Affinity Diagram had done its job. We could now use these new-found categories to create projects to tackle our low morale issue.

To sum up:

1. Write ideas on individual pieces of paper.
2. Group like-ideas together.
3. Name categories.
4. Use categories to structure action plans.

Tool/Framework 5 - Control Charts

"This Walter Shewhart tool is also one of my favorites, Granddaughter. On most farms, the highest paid farmhands are in the habit of repeatedly asking the lower ranks if they are hitting 'their numbers,' for that numbers seem to be all they see. If a number is off by any amount, they immediately launch a grand inquisition to find the cause of that deviation. It is all hands on deck and everyone drops whatever they are doing to find the surface root cause as quickly as possible, definitely not the TDRC, and someone to blame, positively not POUT! Remember Granddaughter that in all processes we encounter in life, there is normal variation. For example, as humans, we do not go to the hospital if our temperature is 0.1 degree above or below normal. It would be a waste of time and resources to investigate the why of that fluctuation and extremely disruptive to the hospital and our daily lives. As for the farm, temperatures recorded in the milk storage room vary between 3 degrees Celsius and 5 degrees Celsius. We set our target at 4 degrees Celsius. When reporting to 'higher ups' that the current temperature is 3.5 degrees Celsius, it does not mean that we are in trouble and it is NOT a call for action. If the temperature reported is 5.1 or 2.9 degrees Celsius, then by all means, yes, we DO need to take immediate action (refer to CAPAR Framework in 'Milkshake' section). Control charts offer peace of mind for the 'higher ups.'

In the example below, we decided to focus on the temperature in the milk storage room at the farm. We had only one call to action at 9:00 a.m.

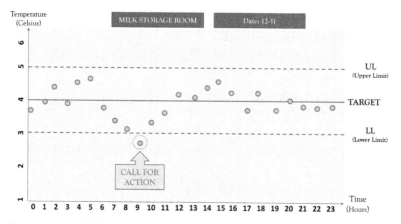

Figure 2.5.1 Milk storage room temperature control chart

In addition, there are some laws of statistics that tell us that we need to evaluate some special patterns for call to action. They are often referred to as "The 8 Control Chart Rules," and live in the world of Statistical Process Control (SPC) but we will save this topic for another day. In conclusion, control charts, when well explained to 'higher ups,' stop the constant fire drills so common in immature, alpha male/female-oriented business culture encountered in the vast majority of the farms on our planet.

To sum up:

1. Educate 'higher ups.'
2. Define the target measure.
3. Define the Upper Limit, if applicable, and the Lower Limit, if applicable.
4. Draw the chart for given reporting frequency (minutes, hours, days, weeks, etc.).
5. Plot data on the graph.

Tool/Framework 6 - Kanban Boards

"This tool, Granddaughter, was rapidly adopted by most of the team at the farm given its ease of use, flexibility, and instant visual reporting. Remember that the location of the board is key to its value. It should be visible for all its intended users without any obstacles. The teams started with the basic design of three columns (To Do, Doing, Done). After a few weeks of practice, some teams adapted the board to fit the uniqueness of their work. In the example below, we decided to use our new Kanban board to manage our improvement of low morale. The first and most simple version of the tool looked like this:

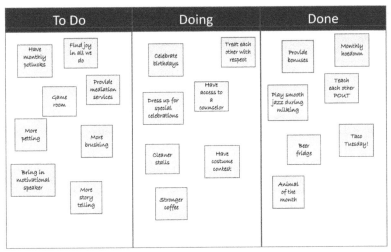

Figure 2.6.1 Simple Kanban board

After a few months, we saw some Kanban boards being used at the team level while other boards were used across teams. These boards looked like this:

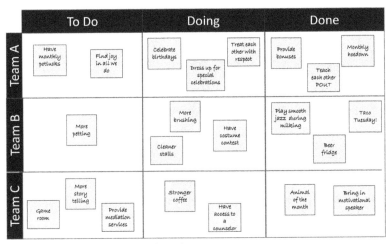

Figure 2.6.2 Kanban board with teams

Or even like this:

	To Do	Plan	Develop	Test	Deploy	Done
Team A	Have monthly potlucks	Dress up for special celebrations		More brushing		Stronger coffee
Team B	Game room		More story telling	More petting	Have access to a counselor	
Team C	Cleaner stalls		Have costume contest / Treat each other with respect	Find joy in all we do	Provide mediation services	Celebrate birthdays

Figure 2.6.3 Kanban board with teams and additional columns

We saw some teams formalize the format of these sticky notes by adding the task (the what), work assignment (to whom), and the due date (by when). Some other teams did not 'stick' to yellow and creatively used other colors to indicate which person had been assigned the 'To Do.' It looked like this:

Figure 2.6.4 Creative use of colors and formats for tasks

To sum up:

1. Select strategic location for the board.
2. Start with simple version.
3. Revise design to best fit the needs of intended users.
4. Keep board current daily."

Tool/Framework 7 - Solution Prioritization Matrix

"For this tool, we must first accept that our minds are far from being rational, Granddaughter. We bring all our biases, conscious and un-conscious, into our decision-making process. At the farm, we use the

Solution Prioritization Matrix to choose the cow, sheep, and farmhand of the month, rank potential options after a POUT exercise, evaluate multiple deep root cause dispositions, select a new cooling system for the milk storage room, and other situations where we have competing alternatives.

In the example below, we opted to work on the selection of a new cooling system for the milk storage room. We had three systems from which to choose. Refer to Figure 2.7.1 at the end of the section for the Solution Prioritization Matrix template.

We had to follow a few steps to set up the tool to evaluate and help us choose the best system. Note that there is no limit to the number of potential solutions to evaluate.

1. Document the name of the solutions being evaluated (replace solutions 1, 2, and 3 with the name of each system) and enter a short description of the system.
2. With the help of the team, list the criteria to be considered in evaluating the options and score each criteria according to importance with 10 = high value and 1 = low value. Document the result in 'Priority.'
3. For each criterion, document the description and value facts associated with each system. For example, if the criterion is cost to acquire, document the costs associated with the purchase of each system.
4. As a team, rate the criteria for each system using 10 as the most favorable and 1 the least favorable. This step is a little tricky. For example, if cost is listed as a criterion, 10 would be used for the least expensive system, whereas if improvement of milk quality/stability is listed as a criterion, 10 would be used for the system that has the highest potential for milk quality/stability.

Refer to Figure 2.7.2 at the end of the section for the team's completed Solution Prioritization Matrix. And this is how we installed our Cold Wizard 2000HP wind-powered cooling system (with the highest score of 387) in the milk barn, Granddaughter!

To sum up:

1. Select competing alternatives.
2. Follow the instructions (step 1 to 4 above) in a team setting.
3. Select the solution with the highest score."

The highest value wins.

Solution Prioritization Matrix

Criterion	Priority	Solution 1			Solution 2			Solution 3		
		Description	Score (1 to 10)	Sub-total	Description	Score (1 to 10)	Sub-total	Description	Score (1 to 10)	Sub-total
		Description			Description			Description		
Total				0			0			0

Figure 2.7.1 Solution prioritization matrix template

Solution Prioritization Matrix

The highest value wins.

Criterion	Priority	Super Cool 5000-X			Refrigeration-R-US			Cold Wizard 2000HP		
		System is powered via electricity. It is installed on the floor of the area to cool. It is all contained inside.	Score (1 to 10)	Sub-total	System is powered via propane gas. It is installed on the wall of the area to cool. Gas tank is the only outside component.	Score (1 to 10)	Sub-total	System is powered via wind turbine. It is installed on a window of the area to cool. Wind turbine is the only outside component.	Score (1 to 10)	Sub-total
		Description			Description			Description		
COST										
Cost to acquire	6	Hardware 5,000	10	60	Hardware 6,000	7	42	Hardware 7,000	4	24
Cost to implement	5	Installation 1,000	8	40	Installation 1,500	7	35	Installation 1,500	6	30
Cost to integrate with structure	5	Construction 800	8	40	Construction 1200	7	35	Construction 1,300	6	30
Cost of maintenance of system	8	Annual maintenance 500	5	40	Annual maintenance 600	4	32	Annual maintenance 600	4	32
Cost to run	10	Average yearly energy cost 10,000	1	10	Average yearly energy cost 5,000	5	50	Average yearly energy cost 500	10	100
TIME										
Time to implement	5	30 Days	5	25	40 Days	4	20	40 Days	4	20
RESOURCE										
Resource level	3	3 Farmhands, 1 contractor, 2 cows	3	9	4 Farmhands, 1 contractor, 4 sheep	3	9	1 Contractor, 6 sheep, 4 cows	6	18
Training efforts	2	10 Hours	5	10	12 Hours	4	8	12 Hours	4	8
IMPACT										
Improves milk quality/stability	9	% of passed quality audits 95	5	45	% of passed quality audits 97	6	54	% of passed quality audits 95	5	45
Level of risk if malfunction	10	Yearly time system down hours 48	1	10	Yearly time system down hours 5	8	80	Yearly time system down hours 5	8	80
		Total		289	Total		365	Total		387

1

2 3 4

Figure 2.7.2 Completed solution prioritization matrix

Tool/Framework 8 - Daily Kaizen

"With this tool Granddaughter, the team aimed to create a visual system to capture, manage, and visually display the results of all the small improvements (inexpensive, quick, and easy to deploy) we were considering. It was a way to show everyone's involvement, energize the team, and encourage all to constantly come up with new ideas. We made a rule that every cow, sheep, and farmhand that produced one improvement idea per week would get more hay, longer pasture time, stronger coffee, or extra personal time.

After a few weeks of experimenting with the concept, we developed the following visual for all to see and understand. We called it the 'I DID IT' framework. I DID IT was an acronym that stood for the following:

Table 2.8.1 I DID IT framework acronym and rules

I is for Imagine	See some improvement opportunity? Speak up. Let imagination run wild. Most experienced pains are great sources of improvement. Everyone is empowered. Mistakes are OK as they are the proof that we are trying. Farmhands are coaches and support speaking up.
D is for Discuss	Discuss your idea with a supervisor or farmhand. While all ideas deserve to be heard, they should be evaluated for the following: • Is the idea supported by the team? • Is the idea inexpensive and quick and easy to deploy? • Does the idea pose any risk to the safety of farm inhabitants? • Does the idea cause any undesirable side effects? Capture the situation 'before' the improvement prior to moving to the next step (see I DID IT template, Table 2.8.2).
I is for Implement	Ideas that pass the discussion stage need to be implemented without delay.
D is for Document	Post-implementation, capture and record the situation 'after' the improvement along with its positive effect (see I DID IT template, Table 2.8.2).
I is for Inform	Inform all the other teams of the improvement carried out along with its positive effect.
T is for Tape it	Tape (or tack) the improvement on the barn door for all to see and celebrate.

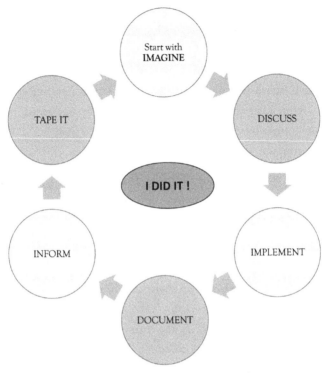

Figure 2.8.1 I DID IT framework

In the example below, we opted to work on the call to the cows and sheep to come to the barn for milking.

Table 2.8.2 I DID IT framework template

Title: Call to the cows and sheep to come to the barn for milking

Before	After
The barn supervisors gather the names of the cows and sheep that are due to be milked and establish a list on a sticky note. They then call 'Batch' and 'Q' to come get the list. 'Batch' and 'Q' go out to the pasture and bark out the names of those on the list requesting their presence in the barn.	*As all cows and sheep already carry a communication device, it is easy for the barn supervisors to gather the names of the cows and sheep that are due to be milked and create an electronic message group. The supervisors send the target message group a text to report to the barn for milking. Cows and sheep on the list are notified with a ring and a buzz and report to the barn.*

Effect				
Lowers the stress level of all the animals in the pasture. Allows 'Batch' and 'Q' to keep herding and protecting the animals. Reduces the time between the call to the barn and the reporting to the barn.				

Name	ID#	Dept ID	Supervisor	Date
Flaky	*009*	*C-003*	*Alaska*	*06-21-20xx*

Some of the keys to success, Granddaughter, is for farmhands, and all those in supervisory roles to lead by example by also putting their ideas through the I DID IT framework. It is by showing commitment and determination regarding new ways of doing things that this tool was adopted. Above all, no one should stop after encountering the first difficulty. Remember, that the new way is here to stay, enshrined in the farm's culture, only after everyone forgets about the old way.

To sum up:

1. Train everyone on the I DID IT Framework.
2. Follow the I DID IT steps.
3. Repeat the process with new ideas."

Tool/Framework 9 - Descriptive Statistics

"What are the binders on the shelves, right there? Are those some kind of tools too?"

"We often collect data at the farm to understand problems better Granddaughter, and the data collection sheets end up in these big binders. The first rule we learned was to always collect data in a random fashion, not choosing and picking. We always drew the names of the farmhands, cows, or sheep that we were going to collect the data from out of a hat. We always collected milk samples at random times. For more complicated 'sampling problems' we went to our Catsultant who would work his magic, informing us of how many samples to choose and the number of people to gather samples from. He called it Sampling Systems and Repeatability and Reproducibility Studies. Catsultant also taught us some basic concepts that we were rapidly able to carry out ourselves, saving us precious catnip.

For example, we wanted to get a better understanding about the amount of time farm inhabitants spent taking phone orders from the cheesemakers. We guessed that some cows, sheep, and farmhands were being overly friendly and chatty, while others were too short and not social enough while taking orders. We simply did not know what our recommendation should be for a not too long and not too short, feel-good phone call.

Per the advice of Catsultant, we decided to collect the time spent for each phone order. Catsultant told us that we should gather data three days in a row from at least three farm inhabitants, randomly selected, every day.

After a week of hard labor, the data collected (phone call length in seconds) looked like this:

Table 2.9.1 *Three days collection of phone call durations*

Date: Oct 3rd-4th-5th												
Location: Office - Main farm building												
Observer: Farmhand Myda A.												
Call duration in seconds												
	Call 1	Call 2	Call 3	Call 4	Call 5	Call 6	Call 7	Call 8	Call 9	Call 10	Call 11	Call 12	Call 13
Day 1	252	271	301	288	341	361	293	381	307	335	222	273	374
Day 2	272	323	275	259	344	273	347	360	365	328	474	257	412
Day 3	----*	252	268	283	324	319	225	255	231	315	377	252	351

*Misrouted call from Grandpa

We then worked with Catsultant and his spreadsheet tool to compute a few key statistics. He said we were going to look at the MEAN (also known as average or AVG), the MEDIAN, the STANDARD DEVIATION, the RANGE, the MINIMUM and the MAXIMUM, and the COUNT of values. Catsultant gave us the following definitions:

Table 2.9.2 Definitions of statistical terms

MEAN (or AVG)	The arithmetic mean or arithmetic average is the sum of a list of numbers divided by the number of elements in the list
MEDIAN	The "middle value" in a list so that 50% of the data collected are below the median and 50% of the data collected are above the median
STANDARD DEVIATION	A measure of how much variation occurs throughout a list of numbers when compared to the average (or mean) of the list. Do values of each element vary greatly around the mean or do they remain close to the mean? This is the question standard deviation answers
RANGE	The largest value in a list of numbers minus the smallest value in the list
MINIMUM	The minimum value in a list of numbers
MAXIMUM	The maximum value in a list of numbers
COUNT	The number of elements in a list of numbers

Catsultant showed us how to run the data analysis and descriptive statistics in his spreadsheet tool. By this time we started feeling like real 'Statischickens' and Catsultant said he found that pretty cute. The key statistics for our dataset looked like this:

Table 2.9.3 Key statistics summary

Length of time in seconds	
Mean	308.9473684
Median	304
Standard Deviation	55.89998181
Range	252
Minimum	222
Maximum	474
Count	38

We started to have new insight from our data. On average the calls lasted 309 seconds (rounded up from 308.94), or 5.15 minutes. Half of the calls were under 304 seconds and the other half above 304 seconds. The range of call duration spanned 252 seconds with the shortest call 222 seconds and the longest call 474 seconds. There was a total of 38 calls measured in our sample data. As for the standard deviation, Catsultant explained that we had to complete a few more steps before fully understanding how to make great use of it. Using his mysterious spreadsheet tool, he asked us to list our phone data in one column and order that list from the smallest to the largest value. Then he instructed us to use a function he called normal distribution,[1] also known as 'norm.dist,' in a second column. That 'norm.dist' function used the values from the first column, the mean of 308.94, and the standard deviation of 55.89 seconds. The normal distribution numbers would tell us the probability distribution of the phone call durations on either side of the mean. The curve is shaped like a bell, hence, its name 'bell curve' with most values clustered in the middle of the range (the mean) and the rest tapering off symmetrically toward either end. The results looked like this for the two columns:

Table 2.9.4 Sorted calls duration and norm.dist function

Length of time in seconds	Norm.dist	Length of time in seconds	Norm.dist
222	0.002128895	307	0.007132387
225	0.002310901	315	0.007095004
231	0.002699499	319	0.007022244
252	0.004247542	323	0.006914734
252	0.004247542	324	0.006882606
252	0.004247542	328	0.006733996
255	0.004479776	335	0.006402238
257	0.00463419	341	0.006054872
259	0.004787794	344	0.005862937
268	0.005457366	347	0.005660759
271	0.00566801	351	0.005377844
272	0.005736343	360	0.004703033
273	0.005803643	361	0.00462608
273	0.005803643	365	0.004316816
275	0.00593492	374	0.003625948
283	0.006407848	377	0.003401517
288	0.006652825	381	0.003109769
293	0.006852128	412	0.0013047
301	0.007064953	474	0.000091283
Cont. next column	Cont. next column		

---

[1]Analysis assumes normal distribution with *p* value = 0.261 and *p* > 0.05.

Catsultant showed us how to use a combo chart with a custom combination in his spreadsheet tool. He then instructed us to select both columns from the previous steps. At this point, we were a bit lost until we saw what our phone dataset looked like on our bell curve (refer to Figure 2.9.1 Frequency distribution of call duration, at end of section).

So, we could now see that nearly 70 percent of our phone calls were within 240 and 360 seconds (or 4 and 6 minutes respectively). Catsultant explained that because we did not have any process requirements or specifications, we should establish some. He recommended that we take the mean minus one standard deviation for our lower specification and the mean plus one standard deviation for our upper specification. That is how we decided that our call duration, moving forward, should be between 4 minutes (253 seconds rounded down) for our 'lower spec' and 6 minutes (365 seconds rounded down) for our 'upper spec.'

With these new goals in mind, we sat down with the sheep, cows, and farmhands and developed some phone scripts. Everyone was trained on the new scripts which included how to be courteous while not being overtalkative. The new scripts were implemented without delay. Three weeks later we gathered a new set of data and provided the results to Catsultant. He shared with us that our new bell curve showed that nearly 96 percent of the phone call frequency distribution was now between 253 and 365 seconds. We had successfully squeezed in another standard deviation within the target range. It took us a bit more practice with Catsultant's help to master this tool, but we were so pleased with the insights from our data that all at the farm agreed it was worth it. There was so much more to discover in the world of statistics, but we would rely on our Catsultant's expertise in the immediate future.

To sum up:

1. Establish the sample size.
2. Collect data following random data collection rule.
3. Run analysis to obtain descriptive statistics.
4. Sort list in ascending order in the first column.
5. Run norm.dist function on the sorted list in the second column.
6. Create combo chart with custom combination on the two columns.
7. Mark graph with mean + 1 Std. dev., mean − 1 Std. dev, mean + 2 Std. dev., mean − 2 Std. dev.
8. Draw conclusion and recommendations.
9. Conduct PDCAS (Plan, Do, Check, Adjust, Standardize) cycle."

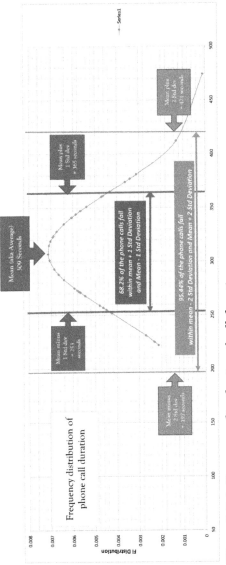

Figure 2.9.1 Frequency distribution of call duration

83

Tool/Framework 10 - Data Cubes: Facts and Dimensions

"The next tool on our 'Whole Milk' list, Granddaughter, was also taught to us by our favorite Catsultant (more catnip please!) on the farm. It was more of a framework for our minds than a tool per se. We often struggled in framing data that contained more than two variables. He started by telling us that there were, more often than not, two categories of data. The first one he called FACT and the second one DIMENSION. Then he added that a third element came into play which he referred to as MEASUREMENT.

Table 2.10.1 Definitions of measurements–facts–dimensions

Measurements	Represents measures such as minimum value, maximum value, sum of values, average of values, count of values, standard deviations, etc.
Facts	Are data to be reported on, such as milk orders, phone call data, sales data, product return, customer complaints, animal health records, rewards awarded, vegetable patch data, etc.
Dimensions	Contain values that support 'dimensions of facts' such as time (hours, days, weeks, months, years), geographic area, farmhand names, sheep names, cow names, animal type, farm fields, farm buildings, types of milk, etc.

Then Catsultant instructed us to use the framework below by first listing all the measurements we were interested in, followed by listing the facts we wanted to report on, and finally listing the dimensions of interest.

The format was MEASUREMENT **of** FACTS **by** DIMENSIONS. Catsultant told us that using '**of**' and '**by**' when setting up the table is key. He gave a few examples:

'I want to look at COUNT (Measurement) **of** PHONE CALL DATA (Fact) **by** CHEESEMAKERS (Dimension).'

'I want to look at SUM (Measurement) **of** MILK DATA (Fact) **by** WEEK (Dimension).'

'I want to look at MAXIMUM (Measurement) **of** CUSTOMER COMPLAINTS (Fact) **by** TYPE OF MILK (Dimension).'

Table 2.10.2 Framework for measurements–facts–dimensions layout

MEASUREMENTS	of	FACTS	by	DIMENSION(S)

After populating the table for the farm, we ended up with the following:

Table 2.10.3 Populated measurements–facts–dimensions layout

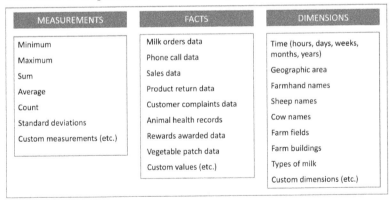

MEASUREMENTS	FACTS	DIMENSIONS
Minimum	Milk orders data	Time (hours, days, weeks, months, years)
Maximum	Phone call data	
Sum	Sales data	Geographic area
Average	Product return data	Farmhand names
Count	Customer complaints data	Sheep names
Standard deviations	Animal health records	Cow names
Custom measurements (etc.)	Rewards awarded data	Farm fields
	Vegetable patch data	Farm buildings
	Custom values (etc.)	Types of milk
		Custom dimensions (etc.)

In the example below, we tried our hand and hooves at answering the question, 'How many sick animals did we have in each field?'

Table 2.10.4 Measurements–facts–dimensions layout and query one

MEASUREMENTS	FACTS	DIMENSIONS
Minimum	Milk orders data	Time (hours, days, weeks, months years)
Maximum	Phone call data	
Sum	Sales data	Geographic area
Average	Product return data	Farmhand names
Count	Customer complaints data	Sheep names
Standard deviations	Animal health records	Cow names
Custom measurements (etc.)	Rewards awarded data	Farm fields
	Vegetable patch data	Farm buildings
	Custom values (etc.)	Types of milk
		Custom dimensions (etc.)

Next, we wanted to look at the average phone call duration for each of our farmhands.

Table 2.10.5 Measurements–facts–dimensions layout and query two

MEASUREMENTS	FACTS	DIMENSIONS
Minimum	Milk orders data	Time (hours, days, weeks, months, years)
Maximum	Phone call data	
Sum	Sales data	Geographic area
Average	Product return data	Farmhand names
Count	Customer complaints data	Sheep names
Standard deviations	Animal health records	Cow names
Custom measurements (etc.)	Rewards awarded data	Farm fields
	Vegetable patch data	Farm buildings
	Custom values (etc.)	Types of milk
		Custom dimensions (etc.)

That was great, but then we were flabbergasted by what Catsultant asked us to do next. He had us pick one measurement, one fact, and as many dimensions as we wished as long as the question made logical sense. He emphasized that the usage of this framework required choosing only one measurement and one fact, yet as many dimensions as we wanted per question asked.

Table 2.10.6 Measurements–facts–dimensions layout and query three

MEASUREMENTS	FACTS	DIMENSIONS
Minimum	Milk orders data	Time (hours, days, weeks, months, years)
Maximum	Phone call data	
Sum	Sales data	Geographic area
Average	Product return data	Farmhand names
Count	Customer complaints data	Sheep names
Standard deviations	Animal health records	Cow names
Custom measurements (etc.)	Rewards awarded data	Farm fields
	Vegetable patch data	Farm buildings
	Custom values (etc.)	Types of milk
		Custom dimensions (etc.)

This time, the data cube framework allowed us to answer the following question, 'What is the total quantity of milk produced by sheep and cows by hour, day, week, month, and year and by type of milk?'"

"Wow, that is so cool Grandpa. Can you show me how it worked for the vegetable patch data?"

"With pleasure, Granddaughter! Let us first follow Catsultant's method and fill in the table for the vegetable patch dataset. We wanted to look at many measurements **of** our 'Patch Data' facts **by** dimensions of time, vegetable type, yield, achieved height, disease resistance, and row number.

Table 2.10.7 Measurements–facts–dimensions layout for vegetable patch

MEASUREMENTS	of	FACTS	by	DIMENSION(S)
Minimum		Vegetable Patch Data		Time
Maximum				Vegetable type
Sum				Yield
Average				Achieved height
Count				Disease resistant
Std. Deviation				Row number

Our vegetable patch data (Facts) was listed in Grandma's notebook. She started hand recording data on April 1st with the first seeding and continued capturing data until the season ended on September 30th. Below is an extract of her journal for the second half of June:

Date	Row	Vegetable type	Yield (Kg)	Disease free	Height (Cm)
June 15	1	Carrots	0	Yes	32
June 15	2	Green beans	0	Yes	120
June 18	1	Carrots	5	No	38
June 18	2	Green beans	0	Yes	125
June 21	1	Carrots	8	Yes	39
June 21	2	Green beans	4	No	130
June 24	1	Carrots	12	Yes	42
June 24	2	Green beans	13	Yes	140
June 27	1	Carrots	6	Yes	44
June 27	2	Green beans	14	No	142
June 30	1	Carrots	2	Yes	45
June 30	2	Green beans	7	Yes	146

Figure 2.10.1 Vegetable patch data journal

With the data from her journal we could select ONE Measurement, ONE Fact, and ONE or MANY Dimensions and answer questions such as:

- What was the maximum (Measurement) yield (Fact) by month (Dimension) and by vegetable type (Dimension)?
- What was the sum (Measurement) of yield (Fact) by week (Dimension) and by vegetable type (Dimension)?
- What was the average (Measurement) disease-free days (Fact) by month (Dimension)?

We had also learned another important lesson; it was best to use the framework before collecting data. This would ensure that we would collect all the data we would need to later report on.

The greatest thing Granddaughter was that this framework worked for all our questions on the farm and beyond!

To sum up:

1. List all the measures of interest.
2. List all the facts of interest.
3. List all the dimensions of interest.
4. Collect data.
5. Pick one measure, one fact, and as many dimensions as desired.
6. Get insight from the data."

Tool/Framework 11 - The 80/20 Pareto Rule

"One challenge we repeatedly faced on the farm, Granddaughter, was how to tackle all the improvement opportunities with set amount of resources. At first we tried to tackle all of them at once! We soon realized that we were not doing quality work by trying to rush through too many initiatives at once. We needed a new tool. Our turtle doves, as observant as ever, told us about the rule of Farmer Pareto and Farmer Joseph (the latter of whom has helped us before). They purred that in nature there was a rule that stated that for many events about 80 percent of the effects come from 20 percent of the causes. This taught us that by focusing on the top 20 percent of the causes we could fix 80 percent of the effects. We started looking at the different data we had gathered and realized it was true for many aspects on the farm:

- 80 percent of our milk sales came from the same 20 percent of our cheesemakers.
- 80 percent of injuries came from the same 20 percent of hazards.
- 80 percent of health issues of our cows came from the same 20 percent of conditions.
- 80 percent of work complaints came from the same 20 percent of the sheep.
- 80 percent of our return products came from the same 20 percent of our cheesemakers.

To illustrate how to use this new knowledge the turtle doves walked us through an example.

In the example below we focused on the various issues we had with milk quality. The quality control audits of our milk over the past 12 months painted the following picture:

Table 2.11.1 Milk quality audit summary

Defect	Category	Observation
Oxidized	Chemical	12
Barny	Absorbed	9
Salty	Chemical	5
Fruity	Bacterial	78
Cooked	Chemical	1
Stale	Absorbed	10
Acid	Bacterial	82
Feedy	Absorbed	14
Medicinal	Chemical	8
Malty	Bacterial	90
Weedy	Absorbed	11
Flat	Chemical	2

The turtle doves instructed us to sort the data using the observation column from large to small and add a new column to capture the cumulative percentages. The new table looked like this:

Table 2.11.2 Milk quality audit summary sorted by observation

Defect	Category	Observation	Cumulative %
Malty	Bacterial	90	27.95
Acid	Bacterial	82	53.42
Fruity	Bacterial	78	77.64
Feedy	Absorbed	14	81.99
Oxidized	Chemical	12	85.71
Weedy	Absorbed	11	89.13
Stale	Absorbed	10	92.24
Barny	Absorbed	9	95.03
Medicinal	Chemical	8	97.52
Salty	Chemical	5	99.07
Flat	Chemical	2	99.69
Cooked	Chemical	1	100.00

The last step was to create a histogram with two data series and select the defect column, the observation column, and the cumulative percent column. Using the turtle doves' spreadsheet, the new chart looked like this:

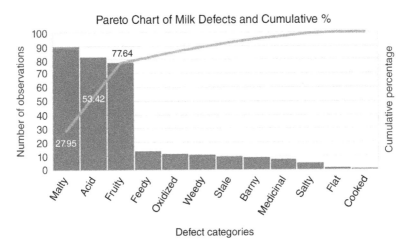

Figure 2.11.1 Pareto chart of milk defects

This chart clearly told us that malty, acid, and fruity were responsible for 77.64 percent of our defects and that they were all associated with a bacterial issue. With the turtle doves' seal of approval, we decided to dig down for the True Deep Root Cause (TDRC) for our repeated bacterial contaminations.

Of course, the 'higher ups' had a hard time letting go of the smaller problems at first as their aim was to look good in the eyes of the other 'higher ups.' Seeing unattended defects on a chart acted contrary to that desire. With time and deeper understanding, they slowly got onboard. They understood that in time, as quality improved, more freed resources would be available to work on the smaller defects.

To sum up:

1. Identify the problematic effects to be studied.
2. Collect or pull data for selected effects.
3. Identify causal categories for the effects.
4. Sort the number of occurrences for each effect in descending order.

5. Add the cumulative percentages.

6. Build the Pareto chart.

7. Define the course of action for the top 20 percent causes."

Tool/Framework 12 - Basic Flowcharting

"Grandpa, I remember the step-by-step work instructions and procedures to describe work, but I wonder if you have a tool to make them easier to understand?"

"That is a great question, Granddaughter. One of the tools we discovered with Farmhand Flo served just that purpose. It was so easy to use that everyone at the farm became proficient in using it within a matter of days. Flo told us that it was called flowcharting. She said the key was to learn four basic shapes. She mentioned that there were more advanced versions of the technique, with many more shapes, but the four we had been taught were all that were needed: oval, rectangle, diamond, and arrow.

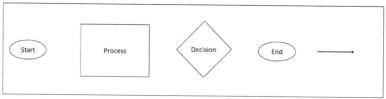

Figure 2.12.1 The four basic flowcharting shapes

The oval has one of two possible labels on the inside, a start label to show where a process starts or an end label to show where a process ends. The rectangle, also known as a process box, is used to describe one step of a process. The label inside always starts with a verb. The diamond is used to show two or more choices. The label inside is a question. The arrow shows the flow of events between shapes. Flo warned us that there were some other rules to follow. One was that a process box, the rectangle, could only have one arrow coming in. Another rule was that a process box could only have one arrow going out. An important decision to make, before trying our hands and hooves at this new tool, was the selection of the level of detail at which we would document a process. A Work Instruction, for example, would be a lot more detailed than a Procedure.

In the example below, we focused on process mapping using a flow-chart for the shearing process of our sheep to serve as a high-level overview for newcomers to the farm. The end result looked like this:

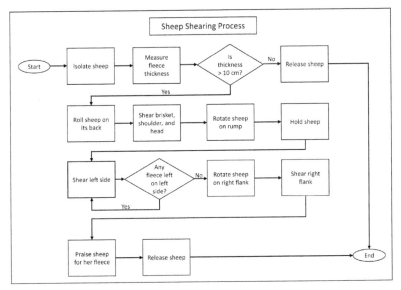

Figure 2.12.2 Sheep shearing process

To sum up:

1. Learn the four shapes and the few rules associated with each of them.
2. Select the desired level of detail.
3. Document the process step-by-step.
4. Review results to ensure rules were applied."

Skim Milk Category

Tool/Framework 13 - RACI

"As the farm grew bigger and more complex, getting organized became more and more difficult, Granddaughter. Many of our projects started with lots of excitement and promises but ended up languishing in the neverland. After critically thinking about our unfortunate project adventures, we realized that several things were happening. The most obvious was that, except for a few, no one knew precisely who was in charge of what. We would sometimes have multiple farm inhabitants working on the same tasks, while other tasks were not being worked on by anyone. It is your Aunt Ethis that came to the rescue. She told us that she had a powerful tool called RACI. She explained that the tool's purpose was to clearly document the roles and responsibilities assigned to project tasks, also known as deliverables. Not surprisingly, RACI was an acronym for the four types of roles and responsibilities.

Table 2.13.1 RACI acronym and definitions

R is for Responsible	Anyone with the 'R' role knew that they were assigned to work and complete a task. For example, 'Batch' and 'Q' were initially responsible for creating the milk production forecast
A is for Accountable	Anyone with the 'A' role knew that they were going to be the one held accountable for the completion of a task. The 'buck stopped with them' and they were the ones calling the shots. For example, the Contractor was accountable for building the new milk storage room according to plans
C is for Consulted	Anyone with the 'C' role knew that they were in an advisory role mostly because of their expertise and experience with a specific task. For example, the turtle doves had to be consulted for anything that related to our milk production flow as they were clearly the experts in that area
I is for Informed	Anyone with the 'I' role knew they were to be kept in the loop as the outcome of a task might impact a task that they were 'R' (Responsible) for. For example, vocal cow was to be kept informed of the progress we made on our Five Whys and TDRC analysis

With the understanding of the four types of roles, Aunt Ethis suggested that we use the format below to list our project tasks and our RACI roles and responsibilities. She said that there was one golden rule to follow: *'for any given task, one and only one resource could be listed as 'A' (Accountable).'*

In the example below, we applied our new knowledge to the 'building of a separate milk storage room' project. The completed template looked like this:

Table 2.13.2 *Completed RACI template*

Indicate (R) Responsible (A) Accountable (C) Consulted (I) Informed		Sponsors and Executives		Project Team			
PROCESS GROUPS	Project: Build separate milk storage room — TASK/DELIVERABLE	Farmer Zeenat	Farmhand Shah	Project Manager Farmhand Linh-Linh	Team Member Mara	Team Member Contractor Angus	Team Member Michelle
Project Initiation	Setup project / project charter	I	C	R/A	I	I	I
Project Planning	Draw plans for temperature-controlled milk storage room	A	ʼ	I	R	C	I
	Contract with specialized construction company	ʼ	A	C	I	R	I
Project Execution	Build room per plan	I	C	I	A	I	I
	Build electrical system	I	C	I	A	I	I
	Build HVAC system	I	C	I	A	I	I
Project Closure	Accept/reject delivery	A	ʼ	I	I	I	I
	Produce project closure documentation	I	I	R/A	ʼ	ʼ	ʼ
	Archive project	I	A	R	ʼ	ʼ	ʼ
Project Control	Execute project management plan	C	I	R/A	I	I	I
	Manage change requests	C	I	R/A	R	I	I
	Manage risk mitigation decisions	C	A	R	I	I	R
	Manage issues / resolutions / decisions	C	A	R	R	R	I

After training everyone on the new tool, we could easily go over the specific roles and responsibilities regarding all of our projects. We added the RACI chart on our visual board for all to see. An extra benefit was the ease it brought to adding or replacing resources on the project, another win-win for everyone.

To sum up:

1. Identify the resource team.
2. List the project tasks in the RACI template.
3. Add the various roles and resources to the RACI template.
4. Work with the team to complete the RACI chart with 'R,' one 'A,' 'C,' and 'I.'
5. Post on visual board."

Tool/Framework 14 - Burn Down Chart

"Do you remember, Granddaughter, when we learned the value of using recipes in the kitchen and in our work?"

"Yes Grandpa, I do remember."

"Well, after we had discovered that secret and had also learned about standard work, we wrote many policies, standard operating procedures, and work instructions. Over time, all the documentation we had written on regular paper started to show signs of wear, and due to the environment on the farm, rot was slowly settling in.

We had to transfer all of the documents to a new farm-friendly support. That was tough news as we estimated we had the following number of documents to convert.

Table 2.14.1 Inventory of documents by document type

	Number of Documents
Policies	20
SOPs (Standard Operating Procedures)	80
WIs (Work Instructions)	110
TOTAL	210

The main challenge was that we had only 30 days (excluding weekends) to get it done as we were getting the farm Quality Certified. At first we struggled to come up with a visual method to track our progress. Tim

Woods was visiting that day and offered to share his knowledge about a tool he called the Burn Down Chart. The tool's purpose was to track work progress over a period of time. It seemed perfect for our needs. Tim worked with us to produce our first version. We had 210 documents to start with and 30 days to reach our objective of having all our documentation updated. That was 210 divided by 30 days, or 7 documents per day. We had no time to lose.

With Tim, we set up our data as follows and started tracking our progress:

Table 2.14.2 Data setup for Burn Down Chart day 1 to 24

Days	Docs daily target	Reverse cumulative daily target	Actual docs daily processed	Balance docs daily processed	Progress balance (cumulative day %) − (cumulative doc processed %)
1	7	210	7	203	0.0
2	7	203	5	198	−1.0
3	7	196	4	194	−2.4
4	7	189	7	187	−2.4
5	7	182	5	182	−3.3
6	7	175	3	179	−5.2
7	7	168	2	177	−7.6
8	7	161	4	173	−9.0
9	7	154	1	172	−11.9
10	7	147	3	169	−13.8
11	7	140	7	162	−13.8
12	7	133	8	154	−13.3
13	7	126	9	145	−12.4
14	7	119	7	138	−12.4
15	7	112	9	129	−11.4
16	7	105	12	117	−9.0
17	7	98	12	105	−6.7
18	7	91	9	96	−5.7
19	7	84	11	85	−3.8
20	7	77	9	76	−2.9

Table 2.14.2 Data setup for Burn Down Chart day 1 to 24 (continued)

Days	Docs daily target	Reverse cumulative daily target	Actual docs daily processed	Balance docs daily processed	Progress balance (cumulative day %) − (cumulative doc processed %)
21	7	70	10	66	−1.4
22	7	63	12	54	1.0
23	7	56	9	45	1.9
24	7	49	9	36	2.9
25	7	42			
26	7	35			
27	7	28			
28	7	21			
29	7	14			
30	7	7			

Then, using Tim Woods' spreadsheet, we created a line chart with markers based on the two columns of 'Reverse Cumulative Daily Target' and 'Balance Docs Daily Processed.' We posted the chart on the team visual board and updated it at the daily team huddles.

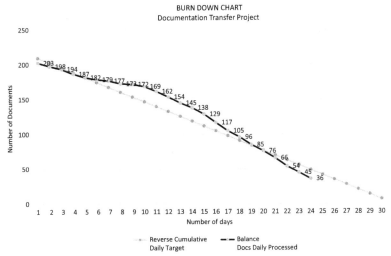

Figure 2.14.1 Documentation transfer project burn down chart

As we went through our project, day by day, we could see that when the dark line was above the gray line, we had to double down and increase the number of documents to process. We also looked at the column labeled 'Progress Balance' that told us by how many percentage points we were from our target. When negative, we were falling behind, when positive we were above our target. This was instant feedback that could be understood by everyone and turned out to be a powerful motivator for the team to rise to this challenge.

To sum up:

1. Collect and analyze the data.
2. Determine the timeline.
3. Build the data table.
4. Build the Burn Down Chart.
5. Place chart and table in very visible area for all to see.
6. Start the project.
7. Update table and chart regularly and religiously.
8. Adjust the daily output to stay on track until the end of the timeline."

Tool/Framework 15 - Critical to Tree

"As we learned to listen to the Voice of Our Cheesemakers (VOCs), we started paying more attention to their wishes. These often sounded quite vague as in 'I want a milk that is good,' or 'customer service is very important to me,' or 'I could use your help in increasing the sales of my cheese.' At first, Granddaughter, we were perplexed as to how to treat these wishes. We recognized these statements were gold nuggets for the farm, but we did not know how to mine them. Our neighbor, Farmer Ben and his wife Emily, were visiting that day and listening in on our conversation. Ben shared with us that he was familiar with a great tool called the Critical to Tree, also known as CTQ or Critical to Quality Tree. He shared the following framework with us:

Figure 2.15.1 Critical to tree framework

In the example below, we focused on translating what two of our most prominent Cheesemakers meant by 'a satisfying glass of milk.' After analyzing the data, we understood that there were three main 'Drivers': the way the milk tasted, the way the milk looked, and the temperature at which the milk was served. These were the 'Drivers.' He then asked us to define the 'CTQ factors' for each driver. For taste, the CTQ factors were creaminess and flavor. For visual, the CTQ factors were color and thickness, and for the temperature driver, the CTQ factor was degrees. There was one final step, Emily said, as she was also familiar with the tool. That was to define the 'Performance Requirements' for each CTQ factor so they could objectively be measured. Once finished, our CTQ looked like this:

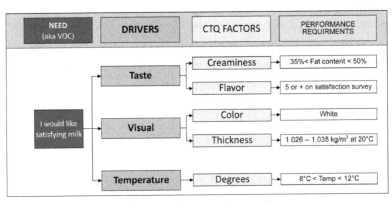

Figure 2.15.2 Critical to tree framework example

Once our tree was completed we could clearly see what needed to be put in place to provide satisfying milk to our cheesemakers in a standard and measurable way.

To sum up:

1. Document one need as expressed by the VOC.
2. Breakdown the need into its Drivers.
3. Breakdown each Driver into its CTQ factor(s).
4. Define the Performance Requirements for each CTQ factor.
5. Develop a plan to fulfill the customer needs."

Tool/Framework 16 - 6-3-5 Silent Method

"After a hard day of labor, Granddaughter, we often sat outside the barn with farmhands, sheep, and cows and engaged in discussions on how to improve our work. Great ideas were generated. We realized that we should find a structured way to harvest the fruits of these reflections. The *Cultivators' Digest* had an insightful article about a tool they referred to as the 6-3-5 Silent Method. The three numbers stood for 6 people, 3 ideas, 5 minutes. The article went on to explain how it worked. It was important to limit the number of participants to a manageable number, anywhere between four and seven was appropriate. The number of ideas set at three was also flexible but was recommended not to exceed five. The time also could vary between 5 and 10 minutes depending on the problem or improvement being discussed. The first step was key to the success of the tool. The participants selected had to be subject matter experts or have a solid understanding of the field being investigated. Participants began with writing a concise problem statement as explained in Chapter 7 'What Causes What by How much?' Then, one idea sheet was distributed to each participant. The idea sheet in the article looked like this:

Problem Statement:

What: Pests on the farm

Cause what : Fruit spoilage

By how much: 30%

IDEA # 1

IDEA # 2

IDEA # 3

Figure 2.16.1 Idea sheet with problem statement

In the example below, we focused on:

What: Pests on the farm

Causes: Fruit spoilage

By how much: 30 percent

We had 4 participants, 3 ideas, and 5 minutes. We set up the exercise as follows:

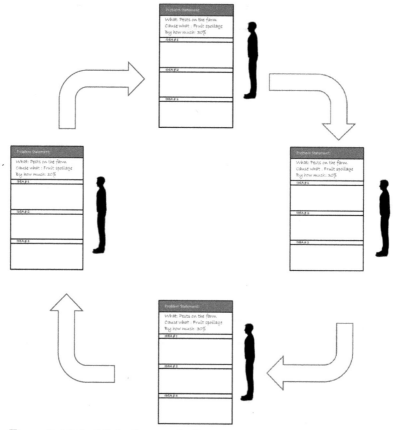

Figure 2.16.2 6-3-5 silent method setup

The next step was to organize as many rounds as we had ideas on the idea sheet, three rounds in our example. In the first round, participants had 5 minutes to document their first idea on their idea sheet. They could draw, write words, or use a combination of both to clearly illustrate their idea. After 5 minutes, each idea sheet was passed from a participant to the colleague on their left. The second round of 5 minutes would then start.

Each participant could consult the previous idea and possibly get inspired by it and write their second idea on the second line of the idea sheet. The third and final round was next, with the idea sheet again being passed to the left and the participants documenting their third idea on the third row of the idea sheet. After the third round was completed, the four idea sheets looked like this:

Problem Statement:
What: Pests on the farm Cause what : Fruit spoilage By how much: 30%
IDEA # 1
Buy and spray pesticides to kill insects and use traps to eradicate other pests
IDEA # 2
Produce organic and only buy and use organic pest control and organic pest repellants
IDEA # 3
Cover trees with nets to protect from Insects

Problem Statement:
What: Pests on the farm Cause what : Fruit spoilage By how much: 30%
IDEA # 1
Stop producing fruit and focus on milk production only
IDEA # 2
Increase biodiversity to figure out which fruits are less prone to bug-eating problems
IDEA # 3
Analyze natural predators of known flying and crawling pests. Then introduce to farm to balance ecosystem

Problem Statement:
What: Pests on the farm Cause what : Fruit spoilage By how much: 30%
IDEA # 1
Place traps to trap insects and pests
IDEA # 2
Pick fruit before maturation and let ripen in temperature-controlled storage room
IDEA # 3
Use a combination of different approaches, nets over trees, organic spray and baits, increase biodiversity etc.

Problem Statement:
What: Pests on the farm Cause what : Fruit spoilage By how much: 30%
IDEA # 1
Bioengineer fruit trees to be pest resistant
IDEA # 2
Use damaged fruit to feed animals
IDEA # 3
Salvage damaged fruit for Aunt Ethis' delicious fruit jams

Figure 2.16.3 Completed idea sheets after all rounds

The final step consisted of going through the ideas and eliminating potential duplicate ideas and merging like-ideas. The cleaned up list looked like this:

- Pesticides and traps
- Organic pesticides and organic traps
- Combination of approaches
- Damaged fruit for jams
- Damaged fruit for animal feed
- Bioengineer fruit trees
- Pick before maturation and ripen in temperature-controlled storage
- Nets over trees
- Introduce natural predators to balance the ecosystem

The logical next step was to feed the list of ideas into a Prioritization Matrix (see Prioritization Matrix tool) to determine which ideas would deliver the most value.

To sum up:

1. Select the number of participants, number of ideas, and the time dedicated for each round.
2. Write the problem statement with the participants.
3. Conduct round one, and then pass idea cards to the left.
4. Conduct round two, and then pass idea cards to the left.
5. Conduct further rounds as needed.
6. Clean up results and generate idea list."

Tool/Framework 17 - Prioritization Matrix

"As the farm grew bigger and more complex, Granddaughter, our list of projects kept growing like wildflowers. We needed to find a way to see which projects should go to the top of our to-do list or to decide if there were projects that we should not work on at all! The challenge was that every team had slightly different criteria in mind when it came to ranking projects. Some viewed 'importance' and 'urgency' as the most relevant criteria, whereas others thought 'value' and 'effort' were more appropriate.

When we asked yet other teams, we discovered new evaluation criteria such as 'value' and 'risk' or 'risk' and 'safety.' It was clear that more criteria could be found based on the intrinsic nature of the work. Farmhand Gerard, who had been part of the conversation all along, said he had seen a tool used in the past when the stakes for freedom were high.

In the example below, we focused on the outcome of a 6-3-5 silent brainstorming we had run to solve the '30 percent fruit spoilage due to pests' problem. As a team, we opted to select 'affordability' and 'effectiveness' as our pair of evaluation criteria. After asking about the priorities on the farm, regarding cost and effectiveness, Gerard drew the following matrix on the wall:

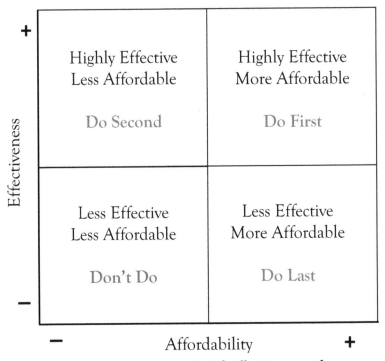

Figure 2.17.1 Prioritization matrix with effectiveness and affordability criteria

We then went to work. We rated each idea 'low' or 'high' for each criterion. For example, 'using damaged fruit to feed animals' was rated 'high' for affordability and 'low' for effectiveness, and 'organic pesticides and organic traps' was rated 'low' for affordability and 'high' for effectiveness.

The team then placed each idea in its respective quadrant. Once done, we stepped back and contemplated the result:

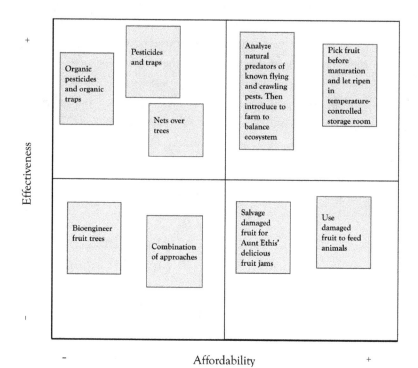

Figure 2.17.2 Completed prioritization matrix with effectiveness and affordability criteria

The two most effective and affordable solutions were to 'pick fruit before maturation and let them ripen in temperature-controlled storage room' and 'analyze natural predators of known flying and crawling pests and introduce to farm to balance the ecosystem.' After conducting Five Whys and Interrelationship Diagrams, it was confirmed that the best way to eliminate the TDRC was to increase biodiversity. We were advised to release lady bugs for the aphids, let loose our ducks in the orchard to eat the snails, install nests to encourage barn owls to inhabit the farm to hunt the pesky gophers, get dogs to watch our chickens, and let the coyotes take care of the moles. While we started journeying down the biodiversity path, we also decided to implement early picking, place nets over our trees, and use organic means to control the pests. We assumed that we would still get some spoilage and that we could use the damaged fruit for jam or animal feed. We all cheered farmhand Gerard for introducing this incredibly insightful tool to the farm.

To sum up:

1. Define the two prioritization criteria.
2. Draw the matrix and place the two criteria on each axis.
3. Based on selected criteria, determine the optimum combination (the 'Do First').
4. Based on selected criteria, determine the next best combination (the 'Do Second').
5. Based on selected criteria, determine the third best combination (the 'Do Last').
6. Based on selected criteria, determine the worst combination (the 'Don't Do').
7. Rate each idea for each criterion using Low and High.
8. Place the projects, improvement ideas, or other items to evaluate in appropriate quadrant.
9. Draw logical conclusions based on visual results."

Tool/Framework 18 - Process Decision Program Chart (PDPC)

"What did you do with very important problems that you could not afford to leave unsolved, Grandpa?"

"That is an interesting question, Granddaughter. Not solving a particular problem could mean shutting the farm down or someone on the farm sustaining an injury. Farmer Andy, our premium catnip supplier, brought us a tool called the Process Decision Program Chart (PDPC) to help us out with such situations. It looked like this:

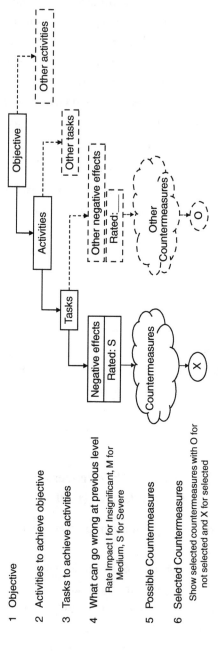

1 Objective

2 Activities to achieve objective

3 Tasks to achieve activities

4 What can go wrong at previous level
  Rate Impact I for Insignificant, M for
  Medium, S for Severe

5 Possible Countermeasures

6 Selected Countermeasures
  Show selected countermeasures with O for
  not selected and X for selected

Figure 2.18.1 Process decision program chart template

Andy added that we should brainstorm as a team for step 4, and that for step 6 we should prioritize the countermeasures and mark which countermeasures made the cut with an 'X' on the chart.

In the example below, we focused on the rodent issue we had in the barn. At night, when most inhabitants on the farm were asleep, rats decided to have some fun in the barn, chomping and chewing on all they could find. With our new knowledge, and Andy's guidance, we worked on our PDPC. After brainstorming and staying late around the firepit for a couple of nights, we produced the following.

We were on our way to successfully managing the risks associated with our objective. That was an effective new tool for our toolshed.

To sum up:

1. Identify critical objectives.
2. Develop the activities to reach the objectives.
3. Breakdown each activity into tasks.
4. Brainstorm for each task reflecting on what can go wrong and document as a negative effect.
5. Rate the impact of each negative effect.
6. Develop possible countermeasures for each negative effect.
7. Select which countermeasures will be implemented.
8. Implement countermeasures and conduct PDCAS (Plan, Do, Check, Adjust, Standardize) cycle."

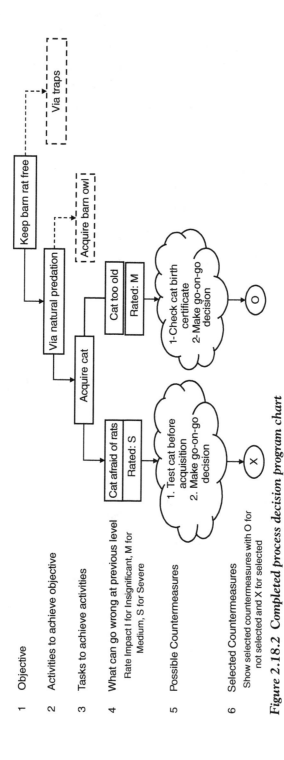

1   Objective

2   Activities to achieve objective

3   Tasks to achieve activities

4   What can go wrong at previous level
    Rate Impact I for Insignificant, M for
    Medium, S for Severe

5   Possible Countermeasures

6   Selected Countermeasures
    Show selected countermeasures with O for
    not selected and X for selected

Figure 2.18.2 Completed process decision program chart

Milkshake Category

Tool/Framework 19 - Theory of Constraints (TOC)

See Chapter 9 – Theory of Constraints (TOC)

Tool/Framework 20 - Corrective Action Preventive Action Response (CAPAR)

"You said that if you combine the tools together they become methods. Can you show me some examples Grandpa?"

"Yes Granddaughter, I will start with one of my favorites called CAPAR. What we discovered about this method is that it works with all undesirable events, large or small. I recall witnessing Aunt Ethis slip and fall on her buttock right in front of the fridge one morning while I was sitting at the breakfast table with Grandma. As she was falling to the floor, almost in slow motion, she exclaimed 'CAPAR!, CAPAR!.' Thankfully, she did not break any bones and was left with only a large bruise. Grandma and I were puzzled by her outburst. We were pressed to ask her what sort of swear word 'CAPAR' was. She laughed hard, but not too hard given her tender backside, and told us that she was going to demonstrate what she meant by 'CAPAR.' After joining us at the table, and deciding to stand rather than sit, she grabbed a pencil and drew the following for us to contemplate:

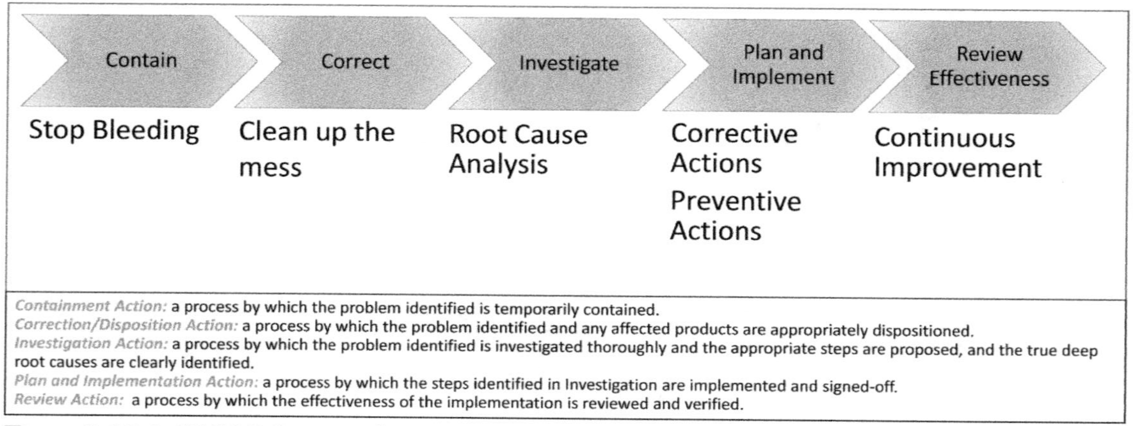

Contain	Correct	Investigate	Plan and Implement	Review Effectiveness
Stop Bleeding	Clean up the mess	Root Cause Analysis	Corrective Actions / Preventive Actions	Continuous Improvement

Containment Action: a process by which the problem identified is temporarily contained.
Correction/Disposition Action: a process by which the problem identified and any affected products are appropriately dispositioned.
Investigation Action: a process by which the problem identified is investigated thoroughly and the appropriate steps are proposed, and the true deep root causes are clearly identified.
Plan and Implementation Action: a process by which the steps identified in Investigation are implemented and signed-off.
Review Action: a process by which the effectiveness of the implementation is reviewed and verified.

Figure 2.20.1 CAPAR framework

She explained that CAPAR was the way to comprehensively address any event with undesirable consequences like the one we had just witnessed. The first step was to CONTAIN. It meant that one of us had to immediately stand by the fridge and warn anyone about the water on the floor so no one else would fall. She referred to this step as 'stop the bleeding.'

The second step was to CORRECT. That meant 'clean up the mess' by mopping and drying the floor. She said most farm inhabitants stop after this second step. We knew, however, that only when the TDRC of a problem was found, could it be eliminated.

So, she went on to say that INVESTIGATE was the next step. In this case, the investigation was quick and simple. Why was there water on the floor? It could have come from the fridge. Looking at the fridge, we saw that the door was properly sealed. We opened the fridge and noticed that the temperature knob was set at '0,' which had forced the fridge to defrost. Because we had not defrosted the fridge in years, the amount of melted ice on the cooling elements was too much for the drainage pan. Water had overflowed causing a puddle to form in front of the fridge eventually resulting in Aunt Ethis' bruised bottom. She asked one more why? Why was the knob at zero? That is when we noticed that we kept our butter dish right next to the control knob. Due to the rectangular shape of the dish, it was easy for it to touch and accidentally rotate the knob to the '0' position.

The next step was PLAN and IMPLEMENT. Since we had found our TDRC, it was time to implement our *corrective action* by resetting the thermostat to '6' where it had previously been. As for implementing our *preventive action*, we agreed that jams would be stored on the right side of the shelf and the butter moved to the top shelf away from the temperature control knob. We tried a few times and saw that due to the round shape of the jam jars, the control knob could not change position inadvertently. We also decided, as another preventive measure, to place the task of defrosting the fridge on our farm equipment maintenance schedule.

Aunt Ethis concluded that the last step of CAPAR was to REVIEW EFFECTIVENESS. We placed a sticky note on the fridge door and wrote the date for the next four Sundays along with the question: 'Has there been water on the floor in front of the fridge in the past week?' We then assigned the task to Grandpa. That was it, and we all yelled loud and clear: 'CAPAR!'

We began using CAPAR whenever we had an event with undesirable consequences. The largest CAPAR we ever encountered at the farm was when we had to recall all of our milk produced over an entire week due to bacterial contamination, that, however, is a story for another time Granddaughter.

To sum up:

1. Notice the event with undesirable consequences.
2. Contain.
3. Correct.
4. Investigate.
5. Plan and implement corrective action.
6. Plan and implement preventive action.
7. Conduct periodic reviews of effectiveness."

Tool/Framework 21 - Project Management

"Grandpa I see a lot of booklets on the workbench."

"You are so observant Granddaughter. These are instruction manuals for the many frameworks we use on the farm."

"When do you use these framework manuals?"

"At first we did not know we needed manuals, but as the little farm grew bigger we could no longer rely solely on the tools we had in the toolshed. It became obvious through our repeated failures that projects had become too complex. We knew there had to be a tool out there that could help us.

At the beginning of one fall season, we had the chance to welcome a visitor from afar, Pierre-Michel de Isambres, or PMI for short. As we were discussing our challenges, he mentioned that there was a great body of knowledge for project management. He called it the PMBOK (pronounced Pimbock). This framework was maintained by many project management professionals from many lands through the Project Management Institute. As we gained experience with more projects we learned that sometimes we could use a light version of the framework for small projects and other times we needed to use the full weight of the framework for very complex or risky projects.

To understand this method Granddaughter, one must first understand that a project is defined as 'a temporary endeavor undertaken to create a unique project, service or result,'[2] and also has a start and an end. Pierre-Michel shared with us that this Project Management Framework relied on a cross between the five process groups and the ten knowledge areas.

---

[2]Project Management Institute. 2017. *A Guide to the Project Management Body of Knowledge.* 6th ed. (Newtown Square: Project Management Institute), p. 4.

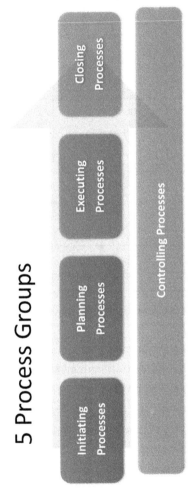

Figure 2.21.1 Five project management process groups

Pierre-Michel told us that projects start with 'Initiating,' move into 'Planning,' followed by 'Executing' and then 'Closing' while being monitored via the 'Controlling' process. He then provided a visual of the 10 knowledge areas:

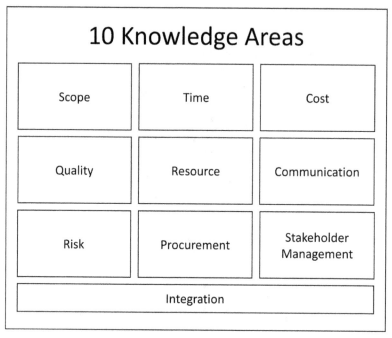

Figure 2.21.2 Ten project management knowledge areas

For each Process Group, there were some prescribed activities that we had to perform. For example, in 'Initiating,' we had to identify all our stakeholders at large impacted by the project. Similarly, in 'Planning,' we had to, among other tasks, estimate our project costs and establish our budgets. We also saw that the bulk of the work in project management happens during the 'Planning' phase. It took us many projects and the help of Pierre-Michel to become good practitioners. I will not go into the details of a complex project, Granddaughter, but wanted you to be aware of this framework and motivate you to learn more from Pierre-Michel de Isambres on your own."

To sum up:

1. Learn about PMI and the PMBOK (get certified!).
2. Practice the framework with a mentor.

Tool/Framework 22 - Problem-Solving in Seven Steps (PS7S)

"With all the tools and framework manuals in your toolshed Grandpa, how did cows, sheep, and farmhands know which ones to use, and when, to solve problems?"

"After we had all learned how to use all of our tools Granddaughter, we realized that every time someone at the farm reported on a new improvement initiative (except for our daily Kaizen that we had standardized) it would sound different. When reporting progress, we always had to spend a few frustrating minutes clarifying at which stage of the improvement project the presenter was. We knew there had to be something better! We needed to have one common way of framing the problem-solving process. This is when the latest issue of the *Cultivators' Digest* pointed us in the right direction. It was not a framework manual per se, but was valuable nevertheless. The article was titled 'Problem Solving in Seven Steps.' It described a structured and chronological method to walk through a process improvement project. In the article, the author stated that all improvement opportunities had to be prioritized first (using a Solution Prioritization Matrix or a Prioritization Matrix) and then fed into the 'Problem Solving in Seven Steps' (PS7S) framework. The 'PS7S' looked like this:

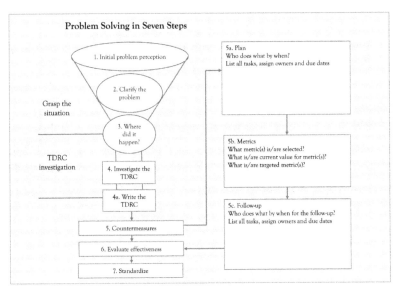

Figure 2.22.1 PS7S framework

After prioritizing our improvement ideas and opportunities, we decided to put the framework to the test. As we had leftover sheep milk on the verge of expiring, we ventured into using this leftover milk for making sweets filled with sheep milk cream liqueur. It was quite delicious. Alaska, after looking at the latest quality control (QC) audit report, declared that there were some problems with the candy wrapping. That was our number one in the PS7S chart, 'initial problem perception.'

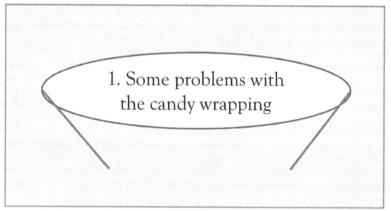

Figure 2.22.2 PS7S framework step one

Since the second step was to 'clarify the problem,' we dove deeper into the QC audit report and discovered that 20 percent of the sweets had a faulty wrapping. They were either torn, overtwisted, or missing entirely! We also found the origin of the defect, the candy wrapping station, to no one's surprise, which was step number three 'where did it happen?' As we were working through the steps of the framework we realized that the content was more important than the form; drawings, sticky notes, small pieces of paper with scotch tape were all fine to use. The article touted content over neatness.

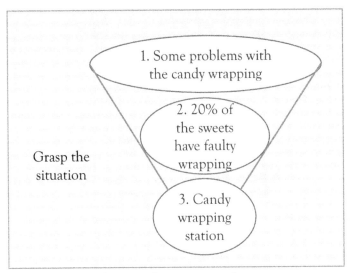

Figure 2.22.3 PS7S framework steps one to three

Step four, directed us to 'investigate and write the True Deep Root Cause (TDRC).' After running through that exercise, we found that the TDRC was the thickness (160 g/m^2) of the candy wrapping material. The excessive thickness of the paper caused a misfeed in the wrapping machine 20 percent of the time.

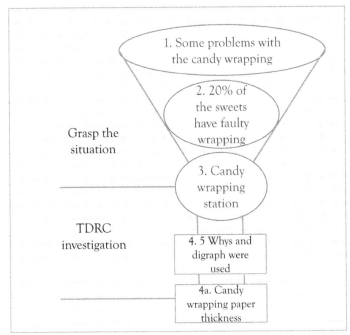

Figure 2.22.4 PS7S framework steps one to four

We were on a roll. Step five instructed us to develop 'countermeasures' by answering the well-known questions:

What? By Whom? By When? The article also directed us to select a metric so we could measure our success.

We were left with steps six, 'evaluate effectiveness,' and seven, 'standardize.' We had to wait to go through the last two steps until after our countermeasures were implemented and the metric 'count of miswrapped candy per 24-hour period' was collected. After evaluating the results against our metric, we found that 100 percent of the candy was wrapped to perfection. We had surely found the TDRC and were ready to standardize by updating any of our documentation that dealt with the wrapping machine such as parts and supply orders, maintenance schedule, etc. The final PS7S looked like this:

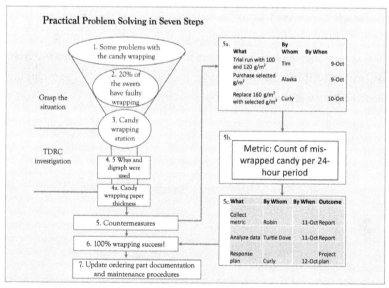

Figure 2.22.5 Completed PS7S framework

To sum up:

1. Teach the framework to all.
2. Complete step 1: Document initial problem perception.

3. Complete step 2: Clarify the problem.

4. Complete step 3: Locate the point/area of cause.

5. Complete step 4: Investigate to find the True Deep Root Cause.

6. Complete step 5: Develop countermeasures.

7. Complete step 6: Evaluate countermeasures against metric.

8. Complete step 7: Standardize.

We found that the PS7S framework worked best for the cows and sheep at the farm. They had limited time to allocate to continuous improvement projects with all the milking and grazing they had to do! The farmhands, however, had more time to spend on analyzing more complex issues. There was a framework called the A3 best suited for that purpose."

Tool/Framework 23 - A3

"What is an A3 Grandpa?"

"An A3 is a single piece of paper that provides a structured, visual, problem-solving framework, Granddaughter. It contains all the parts of a proven, problem-solving methodology. The goal is for the format to be known and used by everyone! It is a great communication tool that fosters dialogue and builds consensus. We found that it was best suited for farmhands rather than cows and sheep, though every farm is different."

"How do you use it, Grandpa?"

"Work all the sections in sequence and report progress as it happens. It is typical and necessary to write in pencil and revisit each section many times! An A3 cannot be completed in one sitting. After each section is worked out, sometimes over the course of days or weeks, it needs to be shared with teammates and farmhands and revised with the information brought forward in the review."

"What are the ground rules for sharing the A3 Grandpa?"

"The first step, after training everyone on the tool, of course, is to get everyone an 11×17 A3 paper template. As the A3 section fills up with progress, A3 owners need to follow a few simple rules:

- When ready to present, the A3 owner distributes copies of the A3 to audience and stands up while presenting.
- Present the A3 straight through to the point of completion.
- Present from the A3, not slides or memory.
- Allow no interruptions, only clarifying questions.
- Each item (box) should contain a graph, chart, or sketch.
- Explain with written words only when a graph, chart, or sketch cannot show the details of the content. It is not about neatness; it is all about content.

We started with the following guide:

A3	Title:		Name:	Date:
I Background Place the problem in its context. Give the big picture. Be factual. Stick figures, hand-written flow charts, drawings work well.		V Proposed Countermeasures What are the various options to reach the target and eliminate the TDRC?		
II Current Condition / Problem Statement What is the problem (what causes what and by how much)? Where are we at with this problem? Use metrics; make it tangible.		VI Plan Draft the plan to eliminate TDRC. Identify who does what by when. List all tasks, assign owners and due dates		
III Goals and Target What end-product are we aiming for? Quantify the goals so we will know if we achieve it.				
IV Analysis This is where we dig for the True Deep Root Cause (TDRC). Use Five whys, interrelationship diagrams, etc.		VII Follow-up Who does what by when for the follow-up? List all tasks, assign owners and due dates		

Figure 2.23.1 A3 guidelines

"Can you give me an example Grandpa?"

"Sure thing Granddaughter. I remember Grandma's A3 when we were working on our milk spoilage issue in the storage room. After about 2 weeks of hard work, gathering data, sharing it with the team, revising, and refining the analysis section by section, this is what Grandma's completed A3 looked like.

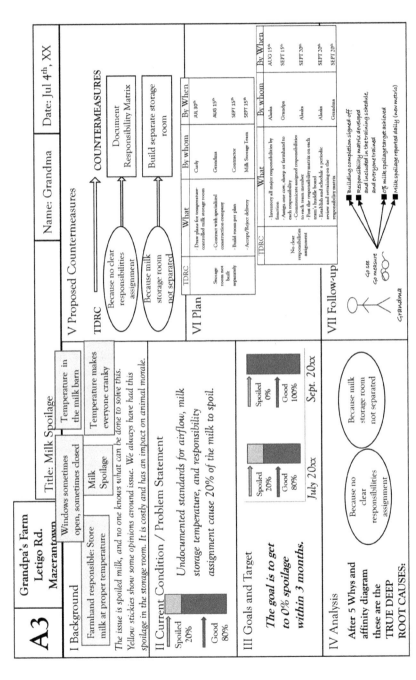

Figure 2.23.2 Completed A3

To sum up:

1. Train everyone on A3.
2. Go through the different sections of the A3 with a mentor.
3. Share the A3 with the team as progress is being made.
4. Repeat with other process improvement opportunities.

So you see Granddaughter how important tools and frameworks are for not only successfully growing a farm but also in fostering the success and fulfillment of its inhabitants."

"I see more than ever before Grandpa. I have learned so much in the last two days and had so much fun with you."

"I also enjoyed your company and every single one of your questions for sure! You must be hungry after all that chatting, listening, discovering, practicing mindfulness, and paddling. Let us walk back to the farmhouse while there is still light in the sky and boil some corn on the cob. We will leave the toolshed door the same as the barn door, always open. Now, make sure that you too are open to expanding your knowledge, practicing all you have learned and teaching the lessons to anyone willing to listen. Never settle for acceptable, always strive for the impossible."

APPENDIX A

Six Sigma Tools Matrix

Not all the tools of the trade are stored in the toolshed. Some tools listed in the matrix below can be sought if a particular need arises.

Six Sigma Tools Matrix	Strategic Planning	Project Planning	Organizing Ideas	Clarifying Direction	Mapping	Correlating	Prioritizing	Identifying Root Causes	Brainstorming	Selecting	Experimenting	Verifying	Quantifying
Affinity Diagram	S		S					S	S				
Concept Definition Worksheet			S							S			
Contradiction Matrix (TRIZ)						X			X				
Control Charts												M	M
CT Tree	S	S	S	S	S								
Descriptive Statistics													M
Design Prioritization Matrix	S						S			S			
Fishbone Diagram	M		M		M			M	M				
5 Whys								S	S				
FMEA		X				X	X	X	X				
House of Quality	X		X			X	X		X				

Figure A.1 Six sigma tools matrix

Six Sigma Tools Matrix	Strategic Planning	Project Planning	Organizing Ideas	Clarifying Direction	Mapping	Correlating	Prioritizing	Identifying Root Causes	Brainstorming	Selecting	Experimenting	Verifying	Quantifying
Hypothesis Testing								X			X	X	X
Idea Generation Worksheet									S				
Interrelations Diagram			M			M	M	M		M			
Is/Is Not Analysis	S		S	S	S				S				
Kano Model			S	S			S		S				
Multigenerational Worksheet	M	M	M	M			M						
PDPC	M	M			M				M		M		
Practicality Scale		M	M	M			M			M			
Prioritization Matrix						M	M			M			

Figure A.1 Six sigma tools matrix (continued)

Six Sigma Tools Matrix	Strategic Planning	Project Planning	Organizing Ideas	Clarifying Direction	Mapping	Correlating	Prioritizing	Identifying Root Causes	Brainstorming	Selecting	Experimenting	Verifying	Quantifying
Process Capability				M								M	M
Project Definition				S									
Pugh Concept Selection Method						X	X			X			
Quad Plot				M		M	M			M			
SIPOC-Plus					M			M	M				
6-3-5 Method									S				
Solution Prioritization Matrix						M	M			M			

Figure A.1 Six sigma tools matrix (continued)

Complexity rating: S, simple; M, medium; X, expert. APPENDIX B

APPENDIX B

Map of the Farm

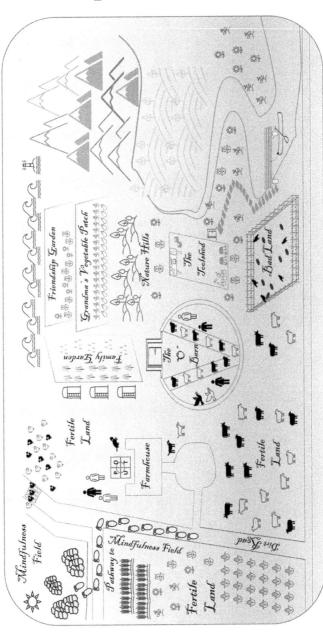

Figure B.1 Map of the farm

Bibliography

Chester, J., and S. Keats. *The Biggest Little Farm*. Documentary Film. Directed by John Chester. New York: Neon, 2018.

Chrissis, M.B., M. Konrad, and S. Shrum. 2011. *CMMI for Development: Guidelines for Process Integration and Product Improvement*. 3rd ed. Boston: Addison-Wesley Professional.

Coelho, P. 2014. *The Alchemist*. San Francisco: HarperOne.

de Saint-Exupéry, A. 1998. *The Little Prince*. Hertfordshire, UK: Wordsworth Editions Ltd.

Fisher, R., and W. Ury. 1983. *Getting to Yes: Negotiating Agreement Without Giving In*. New York: Penguin Books.

Forrester, E., B.L. Buteau, and S. Shrum. 2011. *CMMI for Services: Guidelines for Superior Service*. 2nd ed. Boston: Addison-Wesley Professional.

GOAL/QPC. 2016. *The Black Belt Memory Jogger*. 2nd ed. Methuen, MA: Goal/QPC.

Goldratt, E.M. 1999. *Theory of Constraints*. Great Barrington, MA: North River Press.

Graban, M., and J.E. Swartz. 2012. *Healthcare Kaizen: Engaging Front-Line Staff in Sustainable Continuous Improvements*. New York: Productivity Press.

Groom, W. 2012. *Forrest Gump*. New York: Vintage Books.

Kabat-Zinn, J. 2013. *Full Catastrophe Living: How to Cope with Stress, Pain, and Illness Using Mindfulness Meditation*. London: Piatkus.

Kimball, R., and M. Ross. 2013. *The Data Warehouse Toolkit: The Definitive Guide to Dimensional Modeling*. 3rd ed. Hoboken, NJ: Wiley.

Kotter, J.P. 2012. *Leading Change*. Boston: Harvard Business Review Press.

Krakauer, J. 2007. *Into the Wild*. New York: Anchor Books.

Lenoir, F. 2013. *Du Bonheur: Un Voyage Philosophique*. Paris: Fayard.

Lenoir, F. 2017. *Le Miracle Spinoza: Une Philosophie pour Éclairer Notre Vie*. Paris: Fayard.

Ohno, T. 1988. *Toyota Production System: Beyond Large-Scale Production.* New York: Productivity Press.

Project Management Institute. 2017. *A Guide to the Project Management Body of Knowledge.* 6th ed. Newtown Square, PA: Project Management Institute.

Rother, M., and J. Shook. 2003. *Learning to See: Value Stream Mapping to Add Value and Eliminate MUDA.* Boston: Lean Enterprise Institute.

Shook, J. 2008. *Managing to Learn: Using the A3 Management Process to Solve Problems, Gain Agreement, Mentor and Lead.* Boston: Lean Enterprise Institute.

Trompenaars, F. and C. Hampden-Turner. 2012. *Riding the Waves of Culture: Understanding Diversity in Global Business.* 3rd ed. New York: McGraw-Hill Education.

Ury, W. 2007. *Getting Past No: Negotiating in Difficult Situations.* New York: Bantam Books.

van Vliet, V. 2017. "Taichi Ohno," https://www.toolshero.com/toolsheroes/taiichi-ohno/. (6/22/20).

About the Author

Serge Alfonse, MSc IT, Six Sigma Black Belt, Lean sensei, mediator, and pilot, has accumulated vast business and consulting experience gathered through hundreds of consulting engagements for Fortune 100 companies, thousands of hours as an instructor, and numerous leadership and entrepreneurial positions. Serge started his 30-year career in the field of Enterprise Quality Management before becoming a Six Sigma Black Belt and later a Lean sensei. He developed interests and expertise in the areas of conflict resolution, project management, and company cultural transformation. Throughout his career, Serge has developed courses for City University and various international corporations. His latest role was as Lean sensei and internal consultant for the University of Washington Medical System. Serge enjoys all sorts of outdoor activities, which he is able to engage in frequently as his home is in Seattle, WA, where he lives with his wife Lyne, daughter Camille, two cats, and four chickens.

Index

OTHER TITLES IN OUR SUPPLY AND OPERATIONS MANAGEMENT COLLECTION

Joy M. Field, Boston College, *Editor*

- *Operations Management in China* by Craig Seidelson
- *Logistics Management: An Analytics-Based Approach* by Tan Miller and Matthew J. Liberatore
- *The Practical Guide to Transforming Your Company* by Daniel Plung and Connie Krull
- *Leading and Managing Strategic Suppliers* by Richard Moxham
- *Moving the Chains: An Operational Solution for Embracing Complexity in the Digital Age* by Domenico LePore
- *The New Age Urban Transportation Systems, Volume I: Cases from Asian Economies* by Sundaravalli Narayanaswami
- *The New Age Urban Transportation Systems, Volume II: Cases from Asian Economies* by Sundaravalli Narayanaswami
- *Optimizing the Supply Chain* by Jay E. Fortenberry
- *Sustain: Extending Improvement in the Modern Enterprise* by W. Scott Culberson
- *Managing Using the Diamond Principle: Innovating to Effect Organizational Process Improvement* by Mark W. Johnson
- *Insightful Quality, Second Edition: Beyond Continuous Improvement* by Victor E. Sower and Frank K. Fair
- *The Global Supply Chain and Risk Management* by Stuart Rosenberg
- *Moving into the Express Lane: How to Rapidly Increase the Value of Your Business* by Rick Pay
- *The Effect of Supply Chain Management on Business Performance* by Milan Frankl
- *The High Cost of Low Prices: A Roadmap to Sustainable Prosperity* by David S. Jacoby
- *Sustainable Operations and Closed Loop Supply Chains, Second Edition* by Gilvan Souza

Concise and Applied Business Books

The Collection listed above is one of 30 business subject collections that Business Expert Press has grown to make BEP a premiere publisher of print and digital books. Our concise and applied books are for...

- Professionals and Practitioners
- Faculty who adopt our books for courses
- Librarians who know that BEP's Digital Libraries are a unique way to offer students ebooks to download, not restricted with any digital rights management
- Executive Training Course Leaders
- Business Seminar Organizers

Business Expert Press books are for anyone who needs to dig deeper on business ideas, goals, and solutions to everyday problems. Whether one print book, one ebook, or buying a digital library of 110 ebooks, we remain the affordable and smart way to be business smart. For more information, please visit **www.businessexpertpress.com**, or contact **sales@businessexpertpress.com**

Printed in the USA
CPSIA information can be obtained
at www.ICGtesting.com
LVHW010044080224
771186LV00004B/130